WINDOW BOXES,
PATIOS AND TUBS

WINDOW BOXES,
PATIOS AND TUBS

ROBERT HARDISTY

WARD LOCK LIMITED · LONDON

ACKNOWLEDGEMENTS

The publishers gratefully acknowledge the following agencies for granting permission to reproduce the colour photographs: Pat Brindley (pp. 2, 11, 15, 18, 35, 42, 55 and 63); the Harry Smith Horticultural Photographic Collection (pp. 26, 31, 39, 47, 59 and 78). The remaining photographs (cover picture, pp. 51, 67, 70, 75, 79 and 82) were taken by Bob Challinor.

All the line drawings are by Nils Solberg.

First published in Great Britain in 1987
by Ward Lock Limited, 8 Clifford
Street, London W1X 1RB
An Egmont Company

House editor Denis Ingram

Text filmset in Bembo by
Paul Hicks Limited
Middleton, Manchester

Printed in Portugal

British Library Cataloguing in Publication Data
Hardisty, Robert
    Window boxes, patios and tubs.–2nd Ed.
    1. Container gardening 2. Patio gardening 3. roof gardening
    I. Title
    635.9′86   SB418

    ISBN 0-7063-6508-9

Frontispiece: Wide planters allow several plants to be grouped together in miniature movable landscapes that prevent any patio from becoming predictable.

CONTENTS

PREFACE

I suppose there are still people who think of the garden as that place where there is always work to do, but thank goodness most of us nowadays see it as one of the most pleasant rooms of the house. And who can resist sitting among the plants (provided the weather is favourable of course!). The air is rich with fragrance, and the sound of birds and rustling leaves carries us far away from the town.

Many potential gardeners, however, lack that essential ingredient of cultivation: soil. Their lot is a patch of concrete at one side of their house, or a dull and dreary back yard. But hope is at hand. With just a little imagination and a few pots, tubs, window boxes and plants, your concrete square can be transformed into a lively place of plants and pools.

Gardeners with more room to spare can make their own patio near the house or tucked away among trees and shrubs – a place to escape to.

If you are one of Britian's many flat dwellers all is not lost – window boxes and pots can bring a garden to your doorstep or sill, allowing you to grow a range of flowers and herbs.

So whatever your situation, try bringing a little portable colour to your surroundings; you will find that the minimum of care and attention will result in a generous show of bloom. Patios are not just for the owners of executive ranch-style houses, they are practical proposi-tions for terraced cottages and tiny bungalows. Build one and you will soon enjoy evenings in the twilight, leavened with the scent of barbecued chops and burnt sausages, night-scented stock and nicotiana.

R.H.

CHAPTER 1

PATIOS

Nowadays we tend to glorify any area of paving, concrete or hard standing by calling it a patio, but this Spanish word was originally applied to elegant courtyards within or connected to a house. Whether or not we use the term correctly, it cannot be denied that *our* kind of patio greatly increases the pleasure a garden gives in simple sitting-out terms. What it also does is make it easy to enjoy the garden when it might otherwise be impossible to do so. Sudden summer squalls can soak the lawn, making it quite impossible to move comfortably round the garden for a while until the grass has dried out. But the well-laid patio, given a slight slope or 'fall' to shed water, will soon dry when rain has stopped, making it possible to sit or stand outside with complete comfort at the earliest possible moment.

The garden after summer rain, the sun shining once more, gives the most remarkable pleasure: plant colours appear particularly vivid and the aroma of the wet earth can be deliciously sweet.

The patio might be regarded as an essential adjunct to the house, or at least a highly advantageous feature of it. Quite apart from its direct connections with the garden, it is clearly of immense use when it comes to family gatherings and parties, where a degree of auxiliary space can be valuable in coping with extra bodies.

From a design point of view, the patio can handsomely dovetail the house with the garden, and that is something any appreciative eye will enjoy.

COMMON PROBLEMS

The approach to innumerable houses, both old and new, is rendered mean and difficult by the persistence of many builders in laying narrow front paths which end in the most absurd right-angled offshoot to the front door. Houses afflicted in this way have a job to look their best, and the people occupying them have a very inconvenient and uncomfortable means of entering or leaving.

The rear of the house is often graced with a path approximately one pace wide, immediately next to the building and running from one side to the other. Access to the garden is cramped because of this, and the plot seems to press inwards on the house in a rather uncomfortable manner.

Introduce a patio and all this ends; for here is the means of making the perfect introduction of garden to house and house to garden: an easy spread of well-shaped and well-scaled hard standing taking the place of an inadequate path. Any French windows built into the house at once come into their own.

SIZE

As a general principle, patios are best made larger rather than smaller, commensurate with scale and the amount of room to spare and, of course, funds. It always pays to think patio details right through from the start. Is there going to be enough room for the uses to which it is going to be put? (Garden furniture and a planted tub or two will take up more room than you think.) In any event there needs to be room to enjoy the patio. One that turns out to be poky due to lack of forethought will prove a lasting disappointment.

EDGING

The patio, apart from providing a welcome sitting-out area, also acts as a buffer between the house and the garden. This function is particularly successfully achieved if thought is given to the patio's leading edge. It is always helpful if this steers the line of vision away into the garden. This is, perhaps, best achieved if the leading edge can bow or reach out. This may mean an easy, flowing line if you are using an easily shaped medium such as crazy paving. The patio's leading edge may also be allowed to curve inwards, provided that the distance between the house and the nearest point of the curve is sufficiently great. Here your gaze will be led out into the garden by one or other or both of the outside extremities. Rectangular slabs can always be arranged to drift in order to achieve something of the same aim, even though the effect will be more angular.

Stepping out through the French windows, sliding windows or simply a garden door on to the well-shaped and proportioned patio becomes a pleasure. Just looking at it through the glass will give considerable satisfaction and should extend an irresistible invitation to venture out upon it and into the garden beyond.

Be sure then to give the gaze every opportunity to travel into the garden. What is more, make it easy to walk there too. Do this wherever possible by leaving the leading edge of the patio open and directly connecting with any lawn or continuing garden beyond. If the land rises on leaving the house and a patio has to be cut into the bank, then the principle will have to be modified. In these circumstances push the patio as far forward as possible and make any bank-retaining wall as low as possible to lessen the hemmed-in feeling.

Where land falls away or is level, then there is every opportunity to make the most of the view. So many gardens are made with visual trip-wires right across the line of vision, in the form of flower beds and very often solid walls. The cosy, cloistered feeling may be a deliberately sought effect, but all too often it seems that a frontal 'defence' along the leading edge of the patio is an automatic inclusion. This can just produce a trapped and cramped situation for patio users and a bottled-in and obstructed feeling for those attempting to look at the garden through the house windows. A bed planted with low-growing plants is a better solution if some form of edging is needed.

On the rare occasions where any sort of wall is demanded, then let it be properly scaled in height and general stature, and pushed as far forward as possible.

SHAPE AND SITING

Patios are nearly always constructed as sun-traps, even though the tree- or shrub-sheltered patio with its ferns and fountains is enjoyed by lovers of the shade. The sun cannot always reach the chosen sitting-out area from one end of the day to the other, and it is often necessary to take deliberate steps to catch every available beam. Patio shape takes on a special importance here.

Keep an eye on the path of the sun before you make the patio. Mark out the area which receives the most sunlight by sticking garden canes into the soil on the edges of the shadows, and then construct your patio to a pleasing design within their confines.

Patio shape can have a considerable bearing on garden design, for it can be very much a starting point for the whole layout. In spite of my preference for curved-fronted patios, straight-edged ones look good in any number of gardens where their leading edges have been adapted. A 'broken' or 'stepped' edge is the answer here, for it breaks the formality of the straight line.

The function of patios at the fronts of houses is different as a rule, but basic principles of design remain the same. Freedom of movement is of prime importance and affects all planting spaces made within any patio. It is wise not to overdo the numbers, nor put the spaces where they will get in the way. Take care to avoid planting in front of doors, sliding and French windows that open on to patios.

USING STEPS

Steps from the house down to the patio may be essential if there is not to be a regular and uncomfortable plunge from the upper level to the lower; steps open up all kinds of opportunities.

Well thought out, scaled and constructed steps have every chance of becoming handsome features. Efficient and functional they must be, but their artistic potential should never be overlooked.

Ideally, steps should have deep treads (the part you walk on) and shallow risers (the upright supports) to make passage up and down as comfortable as possible. All treads look better with a slight overhang.

Steps are given increased elegance if they are built of generous width. This will not only offer maximum freedom of movement, but will also allow urns or planted pots to be positioned on their ends, together with cushions to make instant seats. Steps installed with pure function in mind may well turn out to have built-in discomfort: teetering treads and spine-jerking high risers. Made too narrow they will look mean and insignificant.

Straight treads may be just right, but consider also the possibility of a curved outline which might be instrumental in softening their effect and the appearance of a severe patio.

Where air bricks exist under French window lips, steps made in front will have to have a vent made in the appropriate riser to allow air circulation to continue. This will have to tie in with the working out of riser depth in relation to the overall drop from higher to lower level.

SIDE PATIOS

Side patios, like as not snugly shoe-horned in between house and boundary fence, can be both attractive and functional; and with a wall or fence to offer screening from the front, sunny side patios are extremely successful. There might be an extra chance of being overlooked, but this is a hazard that can be overcome by cunning planting to produce a delightfully private and sequestered place for spending lazy days in the sun.

Trough and sink gardens don't have to be planted with alpines. Here evergreens and bedding plants such as the bright-leafed coleus are mixed together.

DISTANT PATIOS

Sometimes patios have to be made right away from the house. With luck the chosen spot could be already backed by a suitable wall. The main consideration would then be to construct an adequately large area of hard standing, blending it in with the surrounding garden. This is not difficult with the wealth of plants and shrubs available today.

As such a feature is likely to be seen full on, a little interesting development can take place, possibly in the making of a small ornamental pool, with planted urns or tubs nearby. Any such inventions soften a slabbed area, especially during less attractive seasons of the year.

Fig. 1 The patio can be effectively screened by fencing or screen block walling. The former blends more easily with the garden, but the latter is longer lasting.

Do remember that patios standing independently anywhere within the garden blend in easily with their surroundings. Choosing the right shape and size will contribute to a successful result.

SCREENS

Backing walls or screens for patios have sometimes to be erected (Fig. 1). They may be built of natural or reconstituted stone, open screen blocks (which can either be bought ready cast or else constructed at home in plastic moulds), or bricks.

The variation in shades of bricks is quite amazing – anything from plum purple to creamy yellow – but if you buy cheap bricks (known as flettons) these can always be coated with exterior quality paint. White paint will reflect the sun but may be too bright for your liking; darker greens and browns can look very harmonious and will show off flowers and foliage to good effect.

Wall brackets fixed to the brickwork will support pots and baskets of trailing plants, and the wall can be capped with a suitable coping to shed water.

If you shun heavy walls and screens (and they are certainly not cheap to construct) there are more lightweight alternatives. Interwoven fencing, trellis supported by stout posts, and rustic wattle hurdles will all provide effective shelter and a pleasing backdrop, and can act as supports for a number of climbing plants.

Do not forget hedges. They do need twice-yearly clipping but they make excellent windbreaks and screens in a variety of shades and forms. Whatever screen you choose, make sure that it cuts down wind rather than light.

PATIO CONSTRUCTION

Ground must be firm if it is to support a patio. If it is solid and reasonably level, then stone-laying can proceed.

Slabs. Lay stone or concrete slabs quite simply on an 8-cm (3-in) deep raked and levelled bed of sharp sand (Fig. 2). Each slab is settled in its own precise position by tapping it with the handle of a club hammer which can also be used with a chisel and some skill to cut large slabs into smaller pieces. It is best to abut each slab tight up against its neighbour, rather than leaving gaps which have to be grouted. However, a few gaps can be left and filled with soil to provide accommodation for carpeting thymes and other sun-loving sprawlers.

Crazy paving. A three-to-one sharp sand and cement mixture is used as a bed for crazy paving. The bed needs to be 2.5 to 5 cm (1 to 2 in) thick to enable crazy-paving pieces to be jockeyed satisfactorily for level. There may be odd places where thickness has to be adjusted to account for superficial variations in the overall level of the ground (or of the paving if it is a truly random selection). If land can be left as it stands before stone laying, all well and good. Where any digging out is necessary to eliminate irregularities in the ground or to allow for essential fall from house or wall in order to shed rainwater, ground should be steadily chipped out so as to disturb the general solidity as little as possible. Rumbustious, over-eager digging will only cause upheaval and needlessly threaten solidity, making control of levels far more difficult.

There is much talk of rammed hardcore, hoggin, gravel and the like as bases for patios. All are quite unnecessary when patios are being created for general domestic use where the ground is solid and the levels workable. There are, of course, occasions where considerable

Fig. 2 Laying concrete slabs in patio construction. Note that each slab is butted tight against its neighbour, that the slab is settled in the bed of sharp sand by use of the club-hammer handle, and that gaps can be left for carpeting plants.

Spring-flowering tulips always look best when underplanted with other early bloomers such as pansies.

deficiencies in level have to be made up before the patio can be laid. Here the hardcore may well be necessary. When it is used, ram it well, then top it with screened ballast before laying the slabs. There should be no need for the addition of sand if the final level and finish of the base is satisfactory.

Grouting. Remember that grouting in mixtures as a general rule should be dry. Brush the mixture (three parts soft sand to one part cement) in, allowing the moisture rising from below to permeate and set it. It is easier and more practical to brush dry grouting in between paving slabs where unwanted gaps exist, and no messy cement marks will be left on the surface of the stone.

Be sure to have something like sacking, thick paper or heavy duty polythene sheeting on hand with which to cover up newly grouted paving should heavy rain or frost threaten.

Slab laying. The mechanics of slab laying are pretty straight-forward. A great deal of the strain of putting some of the larger rectangular slabs down is removed by 'walking' each individual – rocking it from corner to corner – when propelling it across the ground and into position.

It is best to consider slabs of 60 × 60 cm (2 × 2 ft) as the maximum modules for easy working and aesthetic appearance. Random geometrical shapes are a separate consideration. Resist the temptation to try 90 × 60 cm (3 × 2 ft) slabs. They are remarkably heavy and obstinate to handle and often look ugly when laid.

Levelling. Always lay with an adequate fall away from buildings. Work on the basis of being half a bubble out on the spirit level. The bubble should, broadly speaking, run true when laying stone in a lateral direction, unless there are specific reasons for it not doing so. The patio will then run level from side to side (Fig. 3). Remember that air bricks must be left clear and that the patio must begin from a point below the damp-proof course. Build it above the course and it will act as a bridge for moisture and make the inside of your house damp.

The spirit-level and 'straight-edge' work together for the paver in achieving his fall and general plane. The straight-edge is a reasonably robust piece of wood, say 1·5 m × 10 cm × 5 cm (5 ft × 4 in × 2 in). This is long enough for practical reasons and thick enough to remain

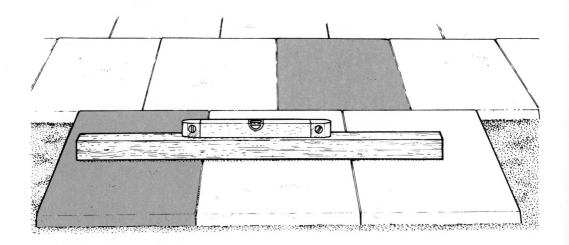

Fig. 3 Levelling slabs in patio construction. Note use of a 'straight edge', a robust piece of wood, say 1.5 m × 10 cm × 5 cm (5 ft × 4 in × 2 in), to cover the breadth of three slabs.

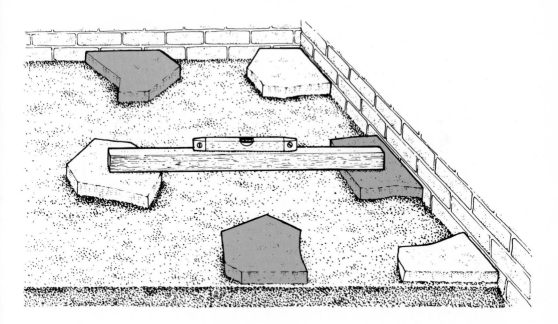

Fig. 4 Crazy paving. Diagram showing the master stones which will determine the run of the finished area. Again note use of a 'straight edge'; also that the tops of the stones are well below the damp-proof course.

rigid and true. It is along this piece of wood, as it runs across master stones and the general area of paving as it progresses, that the spirit-level is laid for checking purposes.

The master stones (or 'spots') govern the run of the crazy-paving patio as it is laid. Complete slabs, if reasonably large, do not require masters as they are big enough to be levelled stone by stone in relation to their neighbours. Because crazy-paving pieces are of such assorted sizes it is far less easy (often impossible) to level them as individuals.

The first few crazy-paving pieces, given the right fall, are laid next to the house. With the aid of the straight-edge and spirit-level, the first master stones are bedded at strategic points (Fig. 4). You can see now why the straight-edge needs to be of reasonable length. It ensures that the master stones are sufficiently far distant to make it easier to get a reliable level, first from the start stones and subsequently between master and master.

If the paving in between masters lies true beneath the straight-edge, which is constantly in use as paving proceeds, then it can reasonably be assumed that the patio as a whole is lying true. The spirit-level, with and without straight-edge, is also in constant use in checking forward and sideways levels of both developing patio and, occasionally, individudal stones. The cement bed is put down progressively and paving pieces tapped level with a club hammer's short handle.

Drain covers. These frequently appear in the middle of patios, just where we do not want them. The ploy of placing a tub or other kind of container – even a bird bath or sundial – on top for disguise is common and remarkably unsuccessful! It does not hide the offending object, but draws attention to it. In ordinary gardens drain covers are fairly easy to lose: borders can be allowed to swallow them up if the border outlines are appropriately altered. Island beds can absorb covers in mid-lawn positions. Plantings of almost any desired kind can then abut the cover to conceal it. Junipers, heathers and some of the low-growing cotoneasters are all good at the job.

Covers in crazy-paved patios pose different problems, but there is an

Don't be afraid to plant daffodils such as 'Carlton' close together. They will make a better show that way and can always be transplanted to the garden after blooming.

easy way out. Pave right up to them, leaving them below the paving level. A simple metal tray of the same dimensions as the cover (which will fit exactly and lie flush with the paving) is next made. This is then placed on top of the cover and made up with crazy paving, grouted in as usual. The thickness of the pieces, on their bed of sand and cement, exactly meets the level of the lip. During the tray-filling process, two wire handles, one at each end, are inserted between the pieces, so that when the grouting dries they are held firm and can be used for lifting the tray out should the pit have to be inspected. Although the rectangular shape of the cover is still in evidence, the crazy-paving in the tray offers exceedingly good continuity with the surrounding paving and, what is more, the patio at this point remains open and uncluttered.

Different textures and colours. The combination of shapes within a patio always adds interest. Crazy paving achieves this, automatically, to a degree. Introducing individual textures and motifs within crazy paving, made from the same or contrasting material, heightens the interest. It pays to work such designs out first. Following this, simple pegging out makes it easy to create individual shapes when laying takes place. The flexibility of crazy paving gives lots of scope, which is why it offers every encouragement for making patios with irregular or flowing outlines, thus avoiding static platforms.

More dramatic changes in texture can be created by laying patches of cobbles or granite setts at intervals (Fig.5). The cement mixture in which cobbles are to be set needs to be on the wet side so that they can be worked in with ease. The straight-edge is also of the greatest use in running across the tops of cobbles as they are laid so that a common level with the surrounding paving is achieved.

Be careful over colours. Neutral tones, especially where space is restricted, are to be preferred. Some of the garishly coloured slabs, particularly when crudely contrasted, can be hard to live with. Neutral tones never jar and are easily enlivened by subtle contrasts – adding a little York stone to ordinary paving slabs, crazy or rectangular, works well – or by planting with or alongside the patio.

Leave strategic stones out at patio laying to create planting pockets and patches. The larger ones will tend to be against house walls and side boundaries for shrubs and climbers.

Sawn-up logs can be sunk into the ground to make a contrasting surface texture, or they can be sunk into flower beds to act as stepping-stones. Do be careful when walking on both logs and cobbles in wet weather for they are inclined to be slippery.

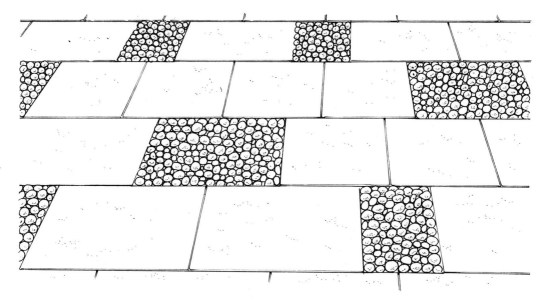

Fig. 5 Changes in texture in patio surface. Here patches of cobbles, set in a cement mixture, relieve the monotony of a paved area. Use the 'straight edge' across the tops of the cobbles to achieve a common level with the paved area.

Single patches can also be created, but these need adroit positioning so that the material is not widely distributed by careless feet. Loose cobbles and pebbles look well and have the advantage of being more difficult to scuff around than shingle. Stepping-stones across shingled areas are attractive, and all manner of patterns can be wrought with pleasingly coloured bricks.

Split levels. Working a change of level into a scheme adds interest. Sometimes this is dictated by circumstances. Where it is not, be sure that there is really room for the development. The construction of raised beds – often a great help to gardeners with stiff backs – or even pools or fountains that can be sat around, will produce features that not only look good but are extremely practical.

Retaining walls. Falling land may necessitate the construction of a retaining wall at the leading edge of a patio in order to achieve a satisfactory level. This feature can be utilized in two ways: it can be planted up, top and sides, with rock plants or trailers, and steps can be built to reach the lower level. Should the steps be built within the patio or extend beyond it? Both propositions have their merits and their possibilities. Steps built within are very neat, save room in the garden beyond and afford yet more casual seating. It just depends on whether there is enough room for them. In any event, the principles of step design mentioned earlier should be borne in mind.

PATIO POOLS

Running water is always associated with tranquillity and restfulness, so what could be more delightful than the gentle trickle of a rivulet of water, or the playing of a fountain on the surface of a patio pool? Constructed of polythene, or made from a pre-cast glass-fibre mould (Fig. 6), the pool is easy to set up and may be either flush with the paving or else raised a little to allow you to sit at the water's edge.

To fit a fibreglass pool into the scene, all you need do is take out the correct-sized hole, insert the pool and then mask the edge with paving stones or a raised brick wall.

Polythene liners will have to be laid on a layer of peat or sand placed in the bottom of a hole which is excavated to the required shape. Water is slowly run in and the liner is flattened against the walls of the pool. When the pool is full, a paved edging can be laid over the protruding polythene to give a neat finish (Fig. 7).

Fig. 6 Pool on patio. A pre-cast glass fibre mould can be built up at the sides with brick or stone, to create a water lily pond as shown.

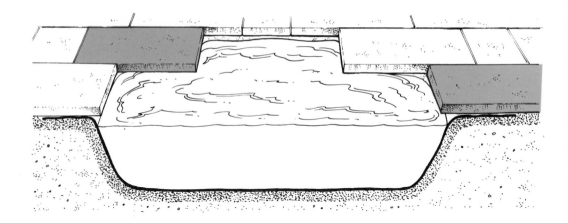

Fig. 7 Pool in patio. Diagram shows cross-section of small pool; a polythene or butyl rubber liner is laid on a layer of sand placed in the bottom and sides of a hole excavated to the desired shape. When the pool has been filled, paved edging can be laid over the protruding polythene as shown.

If all this sounds too much like hard work, why not make a pool from a tub? Sound beer barrels sawn in half (the type that can be obtained from many garden centres) can be coated inside with mastic, positioned on the patio and filled with water. They are usually large enough to support a couple of brilliant goldfish and a miniature waterlily and will prove to be a great talking point.

Around the larger pools a greater selection of plants can be established. Moisture-loving irises and other aquatic plants can be planted in special plastic baskets and submerged in the water. Larger waterlilies can be similarly catered for, and you will discover that the range of pool plants is much larger than you first suspected. Your local garden centre will probably have a good stock of such plants from mid- to late spring – the two best months to start your pool. Do not forget to include underwater oxygenating plants in your scheme so that the fish are kept happy and the water fresh.

MINIATURE GREENHOUSES

If you are tired of paying shop prices for bedding and vegetable plants, why not add a miniature greenhouse to your patio? The structure need not take up much room and it will extend the range of plants you can grow and save you money at the same time.

The miniature lean-to is perhaps the most economical on space. It fits snugly against a warm wall and is equipped with shelves to take pots and trays. Heating can either be accomplished by means of electric air-warming cables, or by installing a small paraffin heater. Even if the structure is not heated at all you can use it for growing bags, full of lettuce in winter and tomatoes, aubergines, peppers, cucumbers and the like in summer.

Provide the greenhouse with a single brick foundation for stability, and make sure that it is firmly anchored to the wall with bolts.

Free-standing miniature greenhouses are also available and these do not feed foundations – one of their advantages is their mobility. Position them in a sheltered spot and move them to a shed or garage in winter to protect them from extreme weather conditions.

Take care to ensure adequate ventilation in all miniature greenhouses in warm weather. They heat up very quickly in spells of bright sunshine and the plants in them may become scorched if not sprayed with water and given plenty of air.Miniature lean-tos are usually equipped with proper ventilators: free-standing greenhouses have sliding glass doors and roof panels which can be raised.

LIGHTING

In good summers, gardens continue to be used until well after dark on warm nights. A little help for the gloaming is both welcome and wise, and outside lighting can be had in abundant variety. The style of lighting will vary according to the needs of the individual, but in any event it should be soundly installed in a proper and professional manner. Correctly set up for outside use, all the equipment will remain durable for the maximum possible time and will, above all, be completely safe.

Concealed lighting, for the patio and its immediate surroundings, has a number of subtle possibilities. Lit after sundown, the patio more than ever becomes a garden room, wrapped round by the night but bright within. Pools and fountains can be lit from above and below water level with plain or coloured bulbs.

Something of a beacon light is very useful to have, attached to the house or to a nearby wall. This will come into its own when paths are trodden after dark. Such service lighting for patio or courtyard is a very worthwhile investment. Powerful enough, it will beam out into the garden beyond. There is real scope for those enthusiastic about moths to install thoughtfully positioned lighting just to encourage these visitors.

GARDEN FURNITURE

There is enough garden furniture about to enable everybody to find something they like. When you come to choose those chairs and that table, however, do make sure that they will fit in with your surroundings, offer the service required of them and as far as possible leave enough room for reasonably free movement all round.

Think also about storage during winter time. If garden furniture has to remain outside the whole year round choose the stout and durable wooden kind which has been treated with a preservative.

Pocket will often enough influence purchase, but it is as well to choose garden seats and tables which combine good appearance with comfort and service. Patio awnings which can be fastened to the side of the house or a wall to give a little shade should also be chosen with taste.

SEASONAL PLANTINGS

In all garden plantings it pays to work towards having something to see and enjoy through the four seasons of the year. This is perfectly easy to arrange. Nursery lists are absolutely full of bulbs, plants, shrubs and trees, it just remains to read the details and choose. Everybody has their favourites but you may find that the display given does not cover the whole year and is not varied enough to provide constant interest.

Winter and its adjacent months are worth giving prime consideration. At such a time it may be difficult to move about the garden, therefore to have real decoration close at hand is a positive delight.

The following plant lists show what you can use around your patio for year-round effect, thus ensuring that there is no closed season.

TREES

To add stature, form and perhaps a little dappled shade to your patio there is nothing to beat a tree. I do not mean an oak or a beech, but one of the smaller ornamental trees whose roots will not disturb paving or house foundations, and whose branches will not fall and smash through roofs. Choose one of the following suggested species that fits in with your plans and your colour scheme.

You can plant at any time of year if your chosen tree is container-grown, between late autumn and early spring if it has been lifted from open ground on the nursery. Prepare the site several weeks in advance, digging the ground thoroughly and working in a little well-rotted compost or manure, plus a few handfuls of bonemeal.

When it comes to planting, take out a hole large enough to accommodate all the roots when they are spread out (unless you are planting a container-grown tree which should be planted with its rootball intact). Drive a stout stake into position immediately before you plant. Inserted afterwards it may damage the tree's roots. Hold the tree in position next to the stake and gradually replace the soil, firming it occasionally with your foot and jarring the tree up and down a little to work the soil particles between its roots. When the tree is planted the mark on the trunk which indicates the old soil level should be in line with the new soil level.

Make sure that the top of the stake finishes a few inches below the lowest branch, and secure tree to stake with two proprietary ties – one at the top and the other at about knee height.

Your patio tree may be surrounded by paving slabs, but cover the area immediately surrounding it (about 60 cm (2 ft) from the trunk) with cobbles, shingle or ground cover plants to allow it a little breathing space

Pruning requirements differ from species to species, but, in general, it is better to thin out overcrowding branches in any tree, rather than to cut them back which will encourage denser, less attractive growth. Many trees of a rather generous size can be kept within bounds by careful annual pruning in winter.

Do remember to site deciduous trees (those which lose their leaves in winter) away from pools which can be fouled with leaves.

Acer palmatum and varieties (Japanese maple). 2–4 m (6–12 ft) high and as much across. Deciduous. Prefers good, well-drained but not dry soil – some will tolerate chalk – and shelter from cold winds. Most varieties have excellent autumn colour.

Good varieties: 'Dissectum', leaves fresh green, finely cut, turning bronze in autumn; 'Dissectum Atropurpureum', leaves deep crimson, finely cut; 'Senkaki', leaves less finely cut than the other two, green becoming bronze in autumn, young twigs bright red through winter. All are relatively slow growing.

Betula pendula 'Youngii' (weeping silver birch). 4.5 m (15 ft) high, 3 m (10 ft) across. Deciduous. Grows well in most soils. Tiny green leaves turning yellow in autumn as they fall. Silvery bark and pendulous branches are attractive all the year round.

Chamaecyparis lawsoniana varieties (false cypress). May grow extremely tall but can easily be kept to 3–4.5 m (10–15 ft) if the top is cut out

when necessary. Evergreen conifer of a columnar shape. Tolerant of a wide range of soils but prefers those which do not get too dry.

Good varieties: 'Ellwoodii', blue-green foliage, slow-growing and not so large as many of its relations; 'Lanei', gold-tinted foliage; 'Grayswood Pillar', grey foliage, tightly columnar habit.

Corylus avellana 'Contorta' (corkscrew hazel). 3 m (10 ft) high, 2 m (6 ft) across. Deciduous. Happy in most soils. The branches are fantastically twisted and carry yellow, trailing catkins in spring. The leaves are coarse and green and tend to mask the decorative branches so the tree is really at its best in winter and spring.

Eucalyptus gunnii (gum tree). Of considerable size but can easily be kept within bounds by pruning. Evergreen. Will grow in a wide range of soils but prefers some shelter from cold winds. Young leaves are round and grey, those on older branches are greener and sickle shaped.

Gleditsia triacanthos 'Sunburst' (honey locust). 10 m (35 ft) high eventually, 4.5 m (15 ft) across. Deciduous. Tolerates a wide range of soils. An elegant tree with pinnate leaves of bright yellow.

Metasequoia glyptostroboides (dawn redwood). Up to 17 m (55 ft) and more, but of a neat columnar habit. Will withstand pruning and even clipping to shape each year. Deciduous. Tolerates all but the driest of soils. The feathery leaves are bright green in summer, turning to rich orange during autumn. This tree is one of our few deciduous conifers.

Prunus 'Amanogawa' (Japanese cherry). 4.5 m (15 ft) (or slightly more) high, but only 1 m (3 ft) or so across. Deciduous. Happy in any well-drained soil. Masses of double pink flowers are carried from mid- to late spring, turning the tree into a column of colour. The leaves follow and are bronzed at first, turning to green as they age.

Pyrus salicifolia 'Pendula' (willow-leaved pear). 4.5 m (15 ft) high, 3 m (10 ft) across. Deciduous. Pleasingly weeping, this tree has narrow grey leaves which glisten in the sun; it is at home in any resonable soil.

Rhus typhina (stag's horn sumach). 4.5 m (15 ft) high and as much across. Deciduous. Tolerates a wide range of soils. Makes a round-

Country gardens need soft-textured containers such as this well-coopered barrel filled with fuchsias, busy-lizzies and ivy-leafed pelargoniums.

headed tree with widely spaced branches. Its long, ferny leaves (deeply cut in the variety 'Lanciniata') are green in summer but turn stunning shades of scarlet, crimson and orange before they fall in autumn.

Robinia pseudoacacia 'Frisia' (false acacia). 9 m (30 ft) high and 4 m (12 ft) across. Deciduous. Thrives in ordinary, well-drained soil. A very elegant tree with bright yellow ferny leaves which are tinged with orange before they fall in autumn.

Sorbus aucuparia 'Beissneri' (mountain ash). 4.5 m (15 ft) or more high and 3 m (10 ft) across. Deciduous. Grows well in most soils but may not do its best on those which contain chalk. This variety is of rather an erect shape and so suited to patio planting. Its leaves are ferny and greenish yellow and the young shoots are red. The bark is coppery orange all the year round but is especially welcome in winter.

SHRUBS

Evergreen and deciduous shrubs are of prime importance in giving your patio form. They are the skeleton upon which the less permanent 'flesh' in the shape of perennials, annuals and so on are hung. Shrubs will provide interest and colour between knee and head height (sometimes higher) and can be planted to contrast with areas of paving, shingle and cobbles. Their colours and leaf shapes can also be associated to good effect.

Planting instructions are the same as those for trees (except that most shrubs will not need staking). The principals of pruning are similar too, except where specific preferences are indicated.

The following is a selection of some of the best patio shrubs, but you will find more under the section on plants for tubs.

Choisya ternata (Mexican orange blossom). 2 m (6 ft) high and as much across. Evergreen. Tolerant of most soils. The shiny green fingered leaves are pungent when crushed. Large bunches of scented white flowers are carried in early summer and often again in early autumn. Though it likes sun the plant will grow almost as well in the shade.

Cistus × *purpureus* (sun rose). 1 m (3 ft) high and 2 m (6 ft) or so across. Evergreen. Will grow well in most soils, even those which are very dry. Large pink flowers, blotched with deep mauve are carried in summer. These plants love the sun and grow well on banks. There are many species with different coloured blooms.

Daphne mezereum (mezereon). 1 m (3 ft) high and as much across. Deciduous. At home in any well-drained soil, even those which contain chalk. Strongly scented lilac-pink flowers are carried up the stems in late winter and early spring. 'Alba' is white-flowered.

Elaeagnus pungens 'Maculata'. 3 m (10 ft) high and 2.5 m (8 ft) across. Evergreen. Likes any reasonable soil which is not too dry. The leaves are oval, edged with dark green and centred with bright yellow. A shrub to bring brightness to your patio all the year round.

Escallonia 'Apple Blossom'. 1.5 m (5 ft) high and nearly as much across. Evergreen. Tolerant of a wide range of soils. This variety is relatively slow growing and has beautiful pink and white flowers in summer. Prune out shoots that have flowered as soon as the blooms fade.

Fatsia japonica (false castor oil). 2 m (6 ft) high and as much across. Evergreen. Thrives in any soil. The massive, glossy, hand-shaped leaves are boldly handsome and contrast well with more fuzzy-textured shrubs. Large white flower heads appear in autumn.

Forsythia intermedia 'Lynwood'. 3 m (10 ft) high and 2 m (6 ft) across. Deciduous. Grows well in any soil. A vigorous shrub with bright green leaves, but these only appear after the bright yellow flowers have had their fling in spring. Prune out shoots that have flowered as soon as the blooms fade.

Lavandula angustifolia 'Hidcote' (sweet lavender). 60 cm (2 ft) high and as much across. Evergreen. At home in any well-drained soil. The grey leaves and the long-stemmed purple-blue flowers are exquisitely scented – particularly in warm sunshine. Clip the bushes lightly when the flowers have faded or been picked.

Mahonia japonica. 3 m (10 ft) high and 2 m (6 ft) across. Evergreen. Tolerant of a wide range of soils. Bold, spiky, pinnate leaves provide all-year-round interest and are topped with pale yellow flower tassels at any time from autumn to spring.

Potentilla 'Katherine Dykes'. Up to 2 m (6 ft) high and as much across. Deciduous. Tolerant of many soils. Deeply cut, small green leaves provide a good background for the many wide-faced clear yellow flowers that are carried in summer.

Santolina chamaecyparissus (lavender cotton or cotton lavender). 60 cm (2 ft) high and as much across. Evergreen. Prefers well-drained soil. A sun-loving shrub with stems that are thickly clad in feathery grey leaves. The plants grow very dense and the leaves are aromatic when crushed.

Senecio 'Sunshine' 1.25 m (4 ft) high and 2 m (6 ft) across. Evergreen. Thrives in any well-drained soil. Another sun-loving shrub with grey leaves which this time are oval and almost white underneath. Yellow daisy flowers are carried in summer. (Often listed in catalogues as *S. laxifolius*.)

Viburnum farreri (syn. *V. fragrans*). Up to 3 m (10 ft) or so high and 2 m (6 ft) across. Deciduous. Prefers good, well-drained but moisture-retentive soil. The plain leaves are shed in autumn and the pinkish white flower clusters decorate the bare branches from late autumn onwards through winter. The blooms are superbly scented.

Weigela florida 'Variegata'. 1.25 m (4 ft) high and as much across. Deciduous. Tolerant of a wide range of soils. Oval leaves of mid-green are edged with creamy white. Rich pink bell-shaped flowers are carried in summer. Prune out shoots that have flowered as soon as the blooms fade.

CLIMBERS AND WALL SHRUBS

For softening bleak walls and for bringing the garden right up to the house, climbers and wall shrubs are very useful. Provide them with support in the form of wires held in position with masonry nails or metal vine eyes, and do not plant them right up against the brickwork where they will become dry at the roots very quickly. Pay attention to watering in dry weather and tie in any wayward branches as necessary.

The plants mentioned here will not do any harm to your foundations or your brickwork, but where self-clinging types such as *Vitis* and *Hedera* are being grown on pebble-dashed walls you would be well advised to put up some kind of framework for them to cling to in addition to the rendering. Should the plants become too heavy they can pull pebble-dashing from the wall. Planting instructions are the same as for shrubs.

As well as preventing weed growth and conserving the moisture in the compost, the pebbles in this planter also show off the inmates to perfection.

Each shrub is indicated as being particularly suitable for walls of certain aspects. The letters at the foot of each entry refer to north-, south-, east-, and west-facing walls.

Camellia japonica and *C. x williamsii*. Up to 2.5 m (8 ft) or so high. Evergreen. Enjoy a moisture-retentive soil enriched with peat. Large, dark green glossy leaves are carried all the year round and large double or single blooms are held above them, usually in spring. The blooms may be white, pink, magenta, scarlet or crimson, and some are contrastingly striped. There are many varieties to choose from. N; W.

Ceanothus 'Autumnal Blue' (Californian lilac). Up to 3 m (10 ft) high. Evergreen. Enjoys ordinary well-drained soil and a sunny spot. Blue powder-puff blooms are carried in late summer and autumn. S; W.

Chaenomeles speciosa 'Moerloosii' (japonica, Japanese quince). 2 m (6 ft) or so high. Deciduous. Tolerant of a wide range of soils. One of many varieties of japonica which flower in late winter and spring, this one has pink and white blossom, others have red, orange, pink or white blooms. N; S; E; W.

Clematis species and varieties. 3–4.5 m (10–15ft) high. Mainly deciduous. Like to have their roots in cool, moist soil. There are many large- and small-flowered varieties with flowers of blue, white, purple, yellow, pink, magenta and crimson. *Clematis montana* has white flowers (pink in the form *rubens*) and is the most vigorous. Choose a colour to match your planting scheme and try twining the plants among other climbers such as honeysuckle (lonicera). N; E; W.

Hedera helix varieties (ivy). Grow to a tremendous height. Evergreen. Will grow in almost any soil. There are plain-leaved and variegated ivies and all will add interest to dull walls. N; E; W.

Jasminum nudiflorum (winter jasmine). Up to 4 m (12 ft) or more. Deciduous. Tolerant of most soils. The arching branches are clothed in bright yellow blooms at any time from late autumn to early spring; the leaves appear later. N; E; W.

Lonicera periclymenum (honeysuckle, woodbine). Up to 6 m (20 ft) but usually less. Deciduous. Tolerates most soils. Oval green leaves are carried all summer on twining stems. The flowers are yellow, tinged with pink, heavily scented and carried from early to late summer. 'Belgica' is early flowering and 'Serotina' late. S; E; W.

Parthenocissus tricuspidata 'Veitchii' (Boston ivy). Grows to a great height. Deciduous. Tolerates any reasonable soil. Sometimes incorrectly called 'Virginia creeper', this plant is self-clinging and carries shiny, maple-shaped leaves which turn rich crimson in autumn before they fall. N; S; E; W.

Polygonum baldschuanicum (Russian vine). Grows as high or as far as you want it to. Deciduous. Tolerates any soil. This extremely vigorous plant grows faster than any other creeper. It has green leaves in summer and foamy white flowers from July onwards. Plant it only when you want fast, dense cover. N; S; E; W.

Pyracantha coccinea 'Lalandei' (firethorn). 4.5 m (15 ft) or more high. Evergreen. Happy in any ordinary, well-drained soil. A thorny wall shrub which has white flowers in summer and orange-red berries in autumn – a good all-rounder. S; E; W.

Rosa varieties (climbing and rambling roses). 3 m (10 ft) and more high. Deciduous. Prefer a good, medium to heavy soil rather than a light, dry one. Available in tremendous variety. Consult specialist catalogues for a good selection. S; W.

Wisteria sinensis (Chinese wisteria). Can reach 18 m (60 ft) and more if supported, but usually much less. Deciduous. Enjoys good soil and flowers better on soils free of chalk. Long, twining stems are clothed in pinnate green leaves all through summer. The flowers, which are lilac-purple in colour, are carried in late spring before the leaves emerge, but there is also a lighter flush of bloom in September. Exquisitely scented. S; W.

GROUND COVER PLANTS
All plants cover the ground to a certain extent, but some do it quicker and more thoroughly than others. The idle gardener, being quick to spot a labour-saving wheeze, has latched on to such plants and spreads carpets of them under trees and shrubs where they can be left to get on with the job of filling a space and smothering unwanted weeds.

This they will most certainly do if you give them a chance, but you must be prepared to hand weed among them in the early stages (probably for a year or two) until they have formed a carpet which weeds find difficult to penetrate. It helps if the ground is well-cultivated, enriched with compost or manure, and made free of weeds at planting time too. Roots of pernicious weeds such as couch grass, dock and dandelion will keep coming up for years if they are not eradicated at the outset.

If you can be a little patient in your gardening and enjoy the carpeting effect as much as the labour-saving angle then you will not be disappointed.

The plants in the following list all look good if they are massed together, but you will also find that clumps of two or three, contrasted with some different foliage, will provide interest too. Remember that not all ground cover plants are evergreen; those that are deciduous or herbaceous (dying down to ground level each winter) will cover the soil only from spring to autumn. All the following plants grow below knee height and some are ground-hugging.

Bergenia (elephant's ears). Large, rounded evergreen leaves will carpet the soil all the year round, though they are fewer in number in winter. Pink or white flowers are carried in spring on stalks which hold them over the leaves. The foliage of some varieties colours up well in autumn. Planting distance: 45 cm (1½ ft).

Calluna (heather). Feathery evergreen foliage which may be brightly coloured in winter. Pink, white or crimson bell-like flowers are carried at any time between late summer and winter. Prefers peaty soil. Planting distance: 23 cm (9 in).

Cotoneaster dammeri. A ground-hugging evergreen with dark green glossy leaves. Carries red berries in summer and autumn. Planting distance: 45 cm (1½ ft).

Erica (heath). Similar to calluna but if anything more feathery in leaf. Pink, white or crimson bell-like flowers are carried at various times of year depending on the variety chosen. It is possible to have flowers all the year round. Prefers peaty soil. Planting distance: 30 cm (1 ft).

Hebe pinguifolia 'Pagei'. Dense domes of neatly arranged evergreen leaves in a pleasant shade of grey are topped with white flower spikes in early summer. Planting distance: 45 cm (1½ ft).

Petunias have long been a favourite of colour-worshipping gardeners. The 'Resisto' varieties are the most reliable for they recover well after summer showers.

Helianthemum (rock rose). Mat-forming evergreen shrubs with small dark green leaves and bright round-faced flowers of yellow, orange, red or white in summer. Enjoy sun. Planting distance: 45 cm (1½ ft).

Hosta (plantain lily). Herbacous perennials which die down in winter. Large fleshy leaves of green, grey-green or green and cream are carried through summer and autumn. Spikes of pale lilac or white bell-flowers are held above the leaves in summer. Bold and showy plants for moist soils. Planting distance 45 cm (1½ft).

Hypericum calycinum (rose of Sharon). An evergreen carpeter of some vigour. It has mid-green leaves and carries bright yellow fluffy-centred flowers in summer. Planting distance: 60 cm (2 ft).

Juniperus (juniper). An evergreen conifer with spreading branches of fuzzy green or blue-grey foliage all the year round. It contrasts well with bold-leaved plants. Planting distance: 1 m (3 ft).

Vinca (periwinkle). Creeping evergreens with dark green leaves and wide-faced flowers of pale blue in spring. Planting distance: 45 cm (1½ ft).

PERENNIALS

There is really no end to the number of perennials or herbaceous plants that you could grow in beds or borders on your patio, but the points to bear in mind when you are choosing them are (*a*) they should not be too large; (*b*) their stems should not be too brittle (for they will be brushed against quite a lot); and (*c*) they should look at home surrounded by paving.

   Prepare the patches of ground that the perennials are to occupy just as you would for other patio subjects – dig or fork it over, add a little well-rotted compost or manure and allow it to settle a while before planting.

   When the clumps become overcrowded they can be lifted and divided before being replanted. The following plants are particularly at home on the patio:

* *Alchemilla mollis* (lady's mantle). 30 cm (1 ft). Pale yellow. Early summer.
* *Artemisia abrotanum* (lad's love). 60 cm (2 ft). Feathery grey leaves.
Euphorbia characias. 1.25 m (4 ft).Green leaves and green flowers. Spring.
* *Geranium* species 45 cm (1½ ft) Blue, white, pink, magenta or crimson. Summer.
Hellebores 30–60 cm (1–2 ft). White or pale green. Winter and spring.

Iris unguicularis. 30 cm (1 ft). Pale to purplish blue. Winter.
* *Polygonum bistorta.* 1 m (3 ft). Pale pink. Early summer.
* *Sedum spectabile.* 45 cm (1½ ft). Pink. Late summer.

Plants marked * die down in winter; the remainder retain their leaves.

ANNUALS AND BIENNIALS

Most annuals are sun lovers and will thrive on sun-trap patios. Which varieties you plant will depend entirely on your own taste, but take advantage of those varieties which are scented, for you will be able to enjoy them that much more when you sit among them. Those which produce their fragrance in the evening are particularly welcome.

Half-hardy annuals are the type that must be raised in a greenhouse (or bought from a nursery or shop as bedding plants in boxes) and planted out when all danger of frost is past in late spring. Hardy annuals are, as their name suggests, more resilient to the weather and seeds of these can be sown outdoors on finely prepared ground in mid-spring. Rake the soil to a fine tilth, scatter the seeds thinly over the surface and lightly rake in the opposite direction. Seeds of one variety can be sown in a drift next to another variety for a particular effect. Thin the seedlings out to a spacing of 15–23 cm (6–9 in) as soon as they are large enough to handle, and support them with small pieces of twiggy branches pushed into the soil.

Biennials take two years to complete their life cycle (unlike annuals which grow, flower and die within twelve months) and are usually sown in rows on a spare piece of ground in early summer. In mid-summer they are transplanted to a wider spacing to allow them room to grow, and are finally transplanted to their final positions in autumn. They will usually bloom the following spring or summer.

Plants such as fuchsias and pelargoniums (geraniums) are really tender perennials and can be lifted at the end of the summer, potted up and protected from frost through the winter. In this way they can be made to last for years. The following list shows some annuals, biennials and tender perennials that enjoy patio life. More detail will be found under the window box and tub sections of this book.

Antirrhinum (snapdragon). 20–100 cm (8–39 in). Mixed colours. HHA.
Calendula (pot marigold). 30–60 cm (1–2 ft). Orange. HA.
* *Cheiranthus* (wallflower). 23–45 cm (9–18 in). Mixed colours. B.
Cleome (spider flower). 1 m (3 ft). Pink. HHA.
* *Dianthus* (sweet william). 15–45 cm (6–18 in). Mixed colours. B.
Digitalis (foxglove). 1–1.5 m (3–5 ft). Pink, yellow and white. B.
Fuchsia. Up to 1 m (3 ft). Mixed Colours. TP.

Gazania. 30 cm (1 ft). Orange, yellow, red and white. HHA.
Godetia. 23–60 cm (9–24 in) Mixed colours. HA.
* *Lathyrus* (sweet pea). 60 cm–2 m (2–6 ft). Mixed colours. HA.
Lavatera (mallow). 60 cm–1.25 m (2–4 ft). Pink or white. HA.
Limnanthes (poached egg flower). 23 cm (9 in). Yellow and white. HA.
Lunaria (honesty) 60 cm (2 ft). Purple, then white pods. B.
* *Matthiola* (night-scented stock). 15 cm (6 in). Pink. HA.
Myosotis (forget-me-not). 30 cm (1 ft). Pale blue. B
* *Nicotiana* (tobacco plant). 30–60 cm (1–2 ft). Mixed colours. HHA.
Pelargonium (geranium). 30–45 cm (1–1½ ft). Mixed colours. TP.
Petunia. 15–30 cm (6–12 in). Mixed colours. HHA.
* *Reseda* (mignonette). 30 cm (1 ft). Orange-brown. HA.
Rudbeckia (coneflower). 60 cm (2 ft). Orange, brown and yellow. HHA.
Tropaeolum (nasturtium). Trailing. Orange, red and yellow. HA.
Verbascum (mullein). 1–2 m (3–6 ft). Yellow or orange. B.
Zinnia (youth and old age)15–45 cm (6–18 in). Mixed colours. HHA.

HA   – Hardy annual
HHA – Half-hardy annual
B   – Biennial
TP   – Tender perennial
*   – Scented

PLANTS FOR RETAINING WALLS AND PAVING

Rock and alpine plants are particularly at home when planted in the top of a hollow retaining wall, and some of them will enjoy the hard life to be found on its sides. Here they will send their roots in search of chinks in the armour, where they can penetrate and gain a foothold.

Not surprisingly, most of these plants demand an exceptionally well-drained medium in which they can grow without fear of becoming waterlogged. The plants on the sides of the wall will manage for themselves, but those growing in the top should be provided with a mixture of good garden soil and fine grit or sharp sand in equal parts. When the wall has been built and the centre has been left hollow, tip a 15-cm (6-in) layer of rubble into the base before filling to within 2.5 cm (1 in) of the rim of the compost.

Plants such as houseleeks (*Sempervivum*) can be attached to the front of the wall by moulding a ball of clay soil around their roots and sticking this to the surface. Gaps in the mortar can be left for plants which are not quite so resilient.

If your retaining wall holds up a bank, you can insert the plants as you build, taking care to ensure that their roots are in contact with a

Grouping several planters of different height relieves the monotony of a flattened planting scheme. When the spring bloomers fade they will be replaced by summer occupants.

pocket of soil which in turn comes into contact with the earth bank.

Once planted in the top of the wall, the chosen plants can be surrounded by a 2.5–cm (1–in) layer of fine gravel or grit to prevent them from being splashed with mud and to keep surface drainage sharp.

Water the plants well in the early stages of development if the soil becomes dry. Those on the sides of the wall will benefit from an occasional visit with the watering can in the drier months of the year.

Several carpeting plants are quite happy to grow in cracks between the paving stones that make up the patio. Here they will look good – breaking up otherwise hard lines – and they do not even mind being walked on; in fact some of them release their perfume more freely when abused in this way. Leave chinks for these plants deliberately; they will thrive with their leaves and flowers in the sun and their roots in the cool, moist soil beneath the paving.

Here are some of the best rock carpeting plants that will enjoy patio conditions:

* *Anthemis* (chamomile). Scented feathery leaves. No flowers in the carpeting form 'Treneague'.
* †‡ *Arabis* (rock cress). White or pink. Spring and early summer. Trailing.
* †‡ *Armeria* (thrift, sea pink). Rich pink. Spring and summer. Hummock forming.
*†‡ *Aubrieta* (purple rock cress). Purple, mauve, pink, lilac or red. Spring and early summer. Trailing.
*‡ *Campanula* (bellflower). Many different kinds with blue, purple or white flowers Spring and summer. Trailing or hummock forming.
* *Mentha pulegium* (pennyroyal). Lilac. Late summer. Trailing or carpeting. Mint-scented when crushed.
*‡*Phlox subulata*. White, pink, red or blue. Spring and early summer. Trailing.
*†‡ *Polygonum affine*. Rich pink. Late summer. Leaves turn bronze in autumn. Trailing or carpeting.
*‡*Saxifraga* (saxifrages). White, yellow, red or pink. Spring and summer. Hummock forming.
*†*Sempervivum* (houseleek). Green, fleshy rosettes often tipped with maroon or covered with 'cobwebs'. Mound forming.
*‡ *Thymus* (thyme). White, pink, crimson or purple. Summer. Carpeting.

* – For gaps in paving
† – For wall sides
‡ – For wall tops

BULBS

Flowering bulbs – particularly those which open their blooms in autumn and winter – are valuable additions to planted beds and borders on the patio. They can be set among shrubs and ground-cover plants, or else planted to replace bedding that has faded, but however you use them, do remember that they enjoy a reasonable piece of soil and a good rest after flowering.

Most bulbs can be left alone when they have bloomed. They will carry on in the same spot for many years, with any luck, if you resist the temptation to cut off their leaves after flowering because they look untidy. Try to resist tying them in bunches, too.

Spring-flowering bulbs should be planted between early and late autumn, autumn flowerers during the summer. As a general rule, bulbs should be covered with soil to twice their depth. For example, a 5 cm (2 in) deep narcissus bulb should be covered with 10 cm (4 in) soil – this means that you will have to dig a 15 cm (6 in) deep hole in which to plant it.

If your bulbs are planted among shrubs you will find them a pleasant surprise at flowering time and quite tolerable when their foliage is looking rather drab afterwards. In such situations they can be left to their own devices. When planted in beds on their own they will have to be lifted and transplanted to another part of the garden after flowering, or else dried off in a cool, dry place, stored and replanted the following season.

There is no end to the variety of bulbs you can plant; here are some of the best:

Chionodoxa (glory of the snow). 15 cm (6 in). White, pink or blue. Spring.
Crocus. 10 cm (4 in). White, yellow, orange, blue, purple. Spring or autumn.
Eranthis (winter aconite). 10 cm (4 in). Yellow. Early spring.
Galanthus (snowdrop). 15 cm (6 in). White and green. Winter and early spring.
Iris reticulata. 15 cm (6 in). Blue mauve or purple. Scented. Spring.
Muscari (grape hyacinth). 23 cm (9 in). Blue or white. Spring.
Narcissus (including daffodils). 15–60 cm (6–24 in). Yellow, white, orange. Early spring.
Nerine bowdenii. 60 cm (2 ft). Pink. Autumn.
Scilla (squill). 10 cm (4 in). Blue or white. Early spring.
Tulip. 15–75 cm (6–30 in). Many colours. Spring.

Bulb catalogues will offer ample choice of variety, and pictures will show the range of colours available.

All kinds of container can be utilized for summer bedding, including redundant wheelbarrows which offer a cool, deep root run.

CHAPTER 2

CONTAINER GARDENING

Be they pots, boxes, bags, troughs or tubs, the portability of planted-up containers is their one big advantage. Many of them are small enough to fit into confined spaces where cultivation would be otherwise impossible, and all of them can brighten up steps, yards, patios and paths which must, of necessity, be hard and unyielding.

The range of containers that can be used in the yard or garden is wide (Fig.8). All sorts of bizarre receptacles can be filled with flowers, but usually the simplest are the most effective.

TYPES

TUBS

There is something cheerful about a tub, most especially the traditional wooden tub; perhaps because of its roundness and solidity. Well coopered, hooped and finished, then granted reasonable maintenance, it has every chance of being a joy for a very long time.

Most good garden centres will sell traditional wooden tubs, either specifically made to be planted up, or else constructed from redundant oak beer casks. Whichever is the case, make sure that the wood is treated with a timber preservative such as Cuprinol inside (and allowed to dry out before being planted up) and with an exterior quality paint or varnish outside. These preparations will ensure that your tub has a long life.

Never use cresote as a preservative for plant containers. It gives off fumes and may even kill the inhabitants of the tub.

Always make sure that your tub has holes in the base to allow free drainage of surplus water. If holes are drilled at 15 cm (6 in) intervals, and a layer of broken flower pots is placed over them before the compost is put in, waterlogging should not be a problem.

Tubs may be made from materials other than wood. Plastic and glass-fibre types are widely available. Many are moulded so that they look like antique lead or stone, and with good-quality workmanship you will have a job to tell the plastic type from the genuine article, even when you are quite close to it.

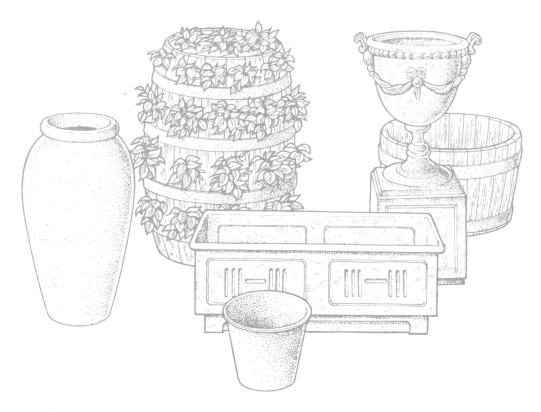

Fig. 8 Containers come in a variety of shapes and sizes. From left, clockwise: an Ali Baba jar; barrel, suitably 'holed' for strawberry plants; wooden tub; urn on pedestal; trough; and terracotta flower pot.

Reconstituted stone tubs look and feel solid and may be just what you need on a busy step or path where lighter containers are likely to be knocked over.

POTS

Terracotta flower pots up to 25 cm(10 in) in diameter are relatively cheap to buy and will support one or more plants depending on their size. A potted geranium will bring cheer to the dullest back step or basement window for next to no expense.

The smaller the container the more quickly it will dry out. If you can only visit your pots once a day in summer, try to use those which are at least 25 cm (10 in) across. Terracotta pots larger than this can be obtained and they are extremely handsome, but they have to be hand thrown, take up much space in the kiln and are consequently much more expensive.

Plastic pots, on the other hand, are relatively cheap, but they always look plastic!

ALI BABA JARS

Guaranteed to bring a touch of eastern promise and class to patio or plot, these terracotta 'oil jars' make a marvellous home for trailing plants which can cast their stems down from the sides. The jars are pricey, but if treated carefully they will last indefinitely. They look good on steps, at the end of retaining walls, and even stood among flowers in a bed or border. As a simple alternative to statuary they are particularly successful.

URNS

Not always ancient Greek in appearance, urns are those bowl-like containers that stand on pedestals. Reconstituted stone, plastic and glass-fibre types are available, and all are more suited to formal patios where they can be arranged singly or in pairs to add height to an otherwise flat area.

Set at either side of a flight of formal steps they certainly add an air of elegance, but used carelessly on a balcony or in a yard they can look extremely ugly!

TROUGHS

Gloomy wall tops and basement paths are easily enhanced with troughs which will fit the area and still allow unrestricted access. Plastic, wooden and stone versions are available and are covered in more detail in the window box section.

SINKS

Rock plants in particular look very much at home in old porcelain sinks which have been teated to resemble stone troughs. This is a job you can do quite easily yourself (Fig.9).

Thoroughly clean the sink and discard the plug (alpines need good drainage so the plughole should be left open!). Coat all surfaces of the sink with a bonding agent such as Unibond or Polybond. When this is tacky your artificial stone mixture can be painted on. Mix up sand, cement and peat in equal parts (only a few trowelfuls of each) and then add water to make a fairly stiff paste. Pat this on to the surface of the sink and allow it to dry.

That's all there is to it. Your sink can be stood on a few bricks, lined with broken flower pots, filled with gritty compost and planted up with rock plants. As the container ages it will become coated with mosses and lichens, so taking on a delightful 'rustic' appearance.

WHEELBARROWS

Although they look rather strange when badly planted up and positioned outside modern public houses, old wooden wheelbarrows

Fig. 9 Stages in making a sink garden.
(a)–(b) Coat all surfaces with a bonding agent, allow to dry and then pat on an artificial stone mixture; (c)–(d) Planting up the sink garden; note use of mixture 'rock' in (c).

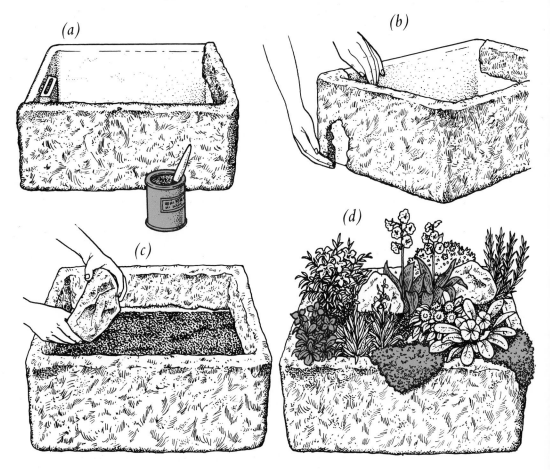

Single-coloured planting schemes can be surprisingly striking. This is *Viola* 'Yellow Crystal' in a stone urn surrounded by lady's mantle and globe flowers.

can add a certain charm to country cottages and yards. When your display is over, all you need to do is wheel the barrow to your working space and fill it up with plants that flower in the next season. Then wheel it back again!

GROWING BAGS

Few people construct patios with the idea of growing vegetables on them, but if you love fresh lettuce or home-grown tomatoes, sweet peppers and aubergines, and have only a patch of concrete, then growing bags can be a real boon.

These plastic sacks are filled with a soilless compost, and slits or holes are usually made in the top at the required spacings to take the crop. Drainage slits are usually made in the base of the sack to allow excess water to escape.

Positioned where they will receive plenty of sun and shelter from strong winds, the bags will produce excellent crops in a relatively small area. Used in the first year for tomatoes or some other demanding crop, the bags can often be retrained for a second season to grow more easily pleased lettuce.

HANGING BASKETS

So far, all the containers I have discussed have had their feet firmly on the ground. But to add what you might call the 'third dimension' to your patio or yard, invest in a few hanging baskets. These containers, suspended from wall brackets, or from screw eyes in pergola cross-members, are always attractive in summer when they are particularly colourful. Wall pots, fixed directly to the brickwork with masonry nails or brackets, are almost as good.

There are a few kinds of hanging basket available; still in the forefront is the type made of concentric wire circles, joined together to form a bowl. This type is unsurpassed in its ability to turn into a solid globe of blossom.

If the basket is to be positioned over a door or path where dripping water would be a discomfort, choose the plastic type of hanging basket which has a built-in drip tray. This basket also has the advantage of not needing a liner to prevent the compost falling out. As hanging baskets need to be prepared rather differently from other containers, it may be a good idea to look at their construction and care here.

Planting up. If you have a traditional wire basket this is the way to plant (Fig.10). Place a pad of sphagnum moss (which you should be able to obtain from the local florist) in the bottom of the basket. Put a

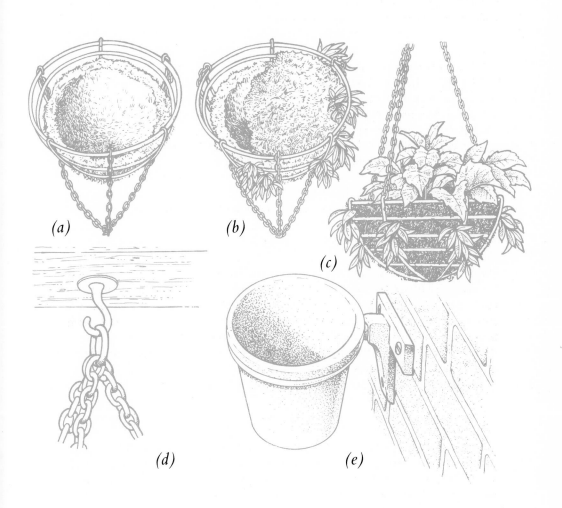

(a)

(b)

(c)

(d)

(e)

Fig. 10 (a)–(c) Making up a hanging basket. First place a pad of sphagnum moss in the bottom of the basket, then place a handful or two of compost on the moss and push two or three trailing plants through the wires. Repeat the process with another series of plants; bushy plants can be placed in the top. (d) Hanging baskets can be hung from hooks screwed into, say, wooden beams.
(e) A wall-mounted pot.

handful or two of compost on top of the pad and push two or three trailing plants through the wires (roots first) at intervals round the basket. Secure them in the compost. With more moss, pad all round and a little way up the inside of the basket, top-up with compost and push in (roots first) another series of plants, reasonably spaced. Secure these with compost as before. Continue this padding round, compost filling and planting process until the top of the basket is reached. Taller and more bushy plants can be planted in the top. If sphagnum moss is not available, use a piece of black polythene as a liner and make slits in it to take the trailing plants.

The plastic hanging baskets fitted with drip trays are not equipped to take plants right up their sides so you will have to content yourself with planting a few trailers around the rim alongside the more bushy subjects that give the planting height.

Hanging baskets are best used only for summer displays. They contain relatively little compost which can freeze solid in winter.

Plants to use in hanging baskets (and for wall pots as well for that matter) include: petunia, nasturtium, alyssum, lobelia, tagetes, fuchsia, geranium, begonia and asparagus fern. Some of the more upright growers, planted on top, will give the basket a nice high centre. (The plant lists at the back of the book give more details.)

Watering. Thoroughly soaked at planting time, baskets should never, thereafter, be allowed to dry out. They may have to be soaked twice a day in the heart of summer.

Occasionally a saucer or small piece of plastic is placed between the initial moss pad and the first handful of compost in the bottom of the basket to stop water from running straight through too rapidly.

Groups of hanging baskets, or indeed wall pots, can profit from drip-delivery watering systems connected to the mains. The water emerges from nozzles set at intervals along a thin, flexible pipe which stretches from basket to basket. Failing this the watering can or hose will do the job efficiently.

HOW TO USE AND CHOOSE CONTAINERS

Bold objects in themselves, tubs and pots exert the most remarkable influence on their surroundings, bringing them to life and opening up

Well-watered hanging baskets will bloom right through the summer. Silver-leafed *Helichrysum petiolatum*, fuchsias and ivy-leafed pelargoniums combine in this one.

opportunities. A dull basement area is given a tub of plants and at once there is a focal point. A patio may be immensely attractive, yet a well-appointed group of flower-filled pots will furnish it with lively colour. However beautifully made, some patios and courtyards look very flat and hard. Containers can provide a change of level sufficient to lift the whole aspect.

As for backyards, the very term strikes a poor sort of note; the pessimistic outlook, a shortage of space, no real room to make anything of a garden. Introduce a tub scaled to fit, position it carefully, plant it brightly, tend it thoughtfully and at once there is hope.

Balconies may be improved by troughs at foot level or maybe parapet height. But there will also be balconies anxious to be freed from straight-sided things. Here a round tub will ease the oblong betwixt building and balcony rail, and offer seasonal displays in welcome, easy-going style. Circular tubs are good at occupying limited spaces. It is being able to walk round them, rather than having to avoid corners, that makes the subtle difference.

Tubs and pots have the most remarkable influence on doors and porches. The formal tub, complete with close-clipped box or bay, seems to add dignity to an entrance, give it elegance and an air of importance, standing sentinel in the face of all-comers. Tops and bottoms of steps are lovely places for adroitly positioned planted pots.

Always choose a container to suit your surroundings. Trying to choose one with essential merit as an object is certainly worth a thought. This does not necessarily mean excess expense, for good design is good design, often amounting to complete simplicity. Certainly some of the most expensive things, on occasions, are the most ugly.

PRACTICALITY

There are practical points to bear in mind when you are choosing containers. Look at depth, width, provision for drainage, sturdiness and colour. I mention sturdiness, for some quite attractive-looking plastic containers tend to bend and bulge when full because they are too thin. Any container should hold its form. Some of the plastic types are a very stark white, which may make them obtrude rather then blend. The textured finish which some of them have tends to trap algae, therefore it is worth making a definite effort to keep them clean. Unlike other materials plastic does not mellow. Becoming dirty is not the equivalent of mellowing.

SIZE

Size of container is important, and the tub or pot chooser has always to bear in mind overall capacity before buying. The container should be able to hold the drainage material, compost and plants comfortably. How the container may fit its allotted space is clearly an obvious proviso too.

PLANTING

The container chosen well is likely to stand as an attractive object in its own right. But planting adds that extra dimension, particularly if it is of the right scale. Small-scale plantings look lost in a large tub; large plantings too domineering in a small pot (putting aside all the difficulties the plants will have in surviving). Plant with an eye to form and balance.

COLOUR SCHEMES

Happy association of colour is a great help, which is why terracotta pots and wooden or plastic tubs and troughs of a reasonably neutral hue thoroughly recommend themselves. They give the plants they contain every chance to look their best.

Container colour becomes particularly important when maintenance comes into focus. Tubs made from stone or manufactured materials which are slow to deteriorate can perhaps be left aside here. But others, principally those of wood, will need attention to help them continue to look their best. An oak tub, clear varnished and black banded, is very handsome. Fresh coats of varnish and black paint, applied every other year are the easy means by which it can not only continue to look in top form, but also survive for the longest period of time.

The trouble starts when painting is preferred. It is not a bad idea, perhaps, to use a subtle shade of green for the overall colour. White-painted tubs do not come amiss. But the use of bright colours needs thinking about very carefully if the plants and flowers are not to be forced into a clashing situation.

There are many garishly painted tubs about, perhaps painted or repainted with whatever spare paint has been available at the time, or maybe given bright coats quite deliberately, the 'artist' quite forgetting that it is not the job of the container to provide the main attraction, but of the plants growing in it. In his genuine enthusiasm he may not realize what a problem he is creating. A good deal of job lot painting seems to go on, too, with house and garage, gates and tubs all the same colour. What a struggle they are going to have to look well.

POSITIONING

The container is right in style, size, shape and colour. The right position has been chosen for it. Next, it needs to be set up prior to being supplied with drainage material, compost and plants. Positioned empty, there is no difficulty arranging and settling it. The mistake can be to fill the container where most convenient and then try to move it into position.

Plant containers find themselves in all sorts of positions for all sorts of reasons. It is nice to have one that can be seen easily from the house; perhaps at a convenient spot on a patio. There is likely to be just the right place on a forecourt, giving the tub and its contents the job of welcoming visitors. There is many an elegant mews or quiet courtyard given that final master touch by an urn overflowing with blooms.

Positions may be sunny or shady. The mobility of a container is such that it can be placed almost anywhere to good advantage. Where there is no real choice, then there are plantings enough to prosper in whatever degree of light may be available, but try to avoid draughty places.

It is best if wooden tubs do not stand completely on the ground. If they do, the drainage water which percolates through, after watering or rain, will tend to become trapped underneath. This is not a particularly healthy situation, and in any case, trapped water is likely to start rotting the bottom rim. The simple and standard answer is to mount the tub on about three pieces of brick so that it is held just clear of the ground. Water will then be able to fall clear underneath and run away. Be sure that the circular edge is sitting fairly and squarely on the brick pieces when the tub is set up. Tubs made with feet will not need to be jacked up in this way.

MOBILITY

It is possible to find tubs and other large containers which run on castors, easing the matter of moving them from one position to another. Such a system might just come to the rescue of a tender plant or shrub needing to be put in a sheltered place for the colder months, but brought out into the open again for the remainder of the year. With tubs held clear of the ground on castors, there is clearly no hold-up in drainage water getting away.

All containers can be moved (using a little careful organization) should certain specimen plantings need to be given shelter during the colder part of the year. Some containers are even made with carrying handles. Over-large tubs will need to be planted wisely, so they never require to be moved for the benefit of their occupants.

DRAINAGE

Most containers for ornamental planting are given drainage holes at manufacture. It is, however, worth taking a look at these arrangements to be certain they are adequate for individual needs. Containers of lesser breeds can sometimes be found with very inadequate drainage arrangements indeed. No doubt, cheapness of production is responsible for this, along with ignorance of the real requirements of growing plants. So it may pay to improve the position by drilling a sensible number of water escape holes.

In all but hole-riddled plastic pots, pieces of broken clay pot, or tile, or brick, are placed in a layer on the bottom to keep the compost sweet

Where flagged or concrete paths offer no root room to plants, troughs can be used to make raised borders.

and drainage holes clear. Rough leaf-mould, or equivalent – someone I knew cut up their old coir doormat into pieces and used that – is placed over the 'brickbat' layer to prevent the planting compost from washing down and clogging the system, while at the same time allowing water to run through. Important as the drainage layers are, they must still leave enough room in the container for a sufficient depth of compost to allow successful growth. Common sense is the guiding influence.

COMPOST

Compost for plant containers should be a properly balanced mixture, so it remains well textured. Unless you are blessed with good soil containing plenty of humus, filling a tub straight from the garden is not the best way to successful culture, as all too often it cakes and sets in a solid lump. John Innes No. 2 potting compost will provide all the nutrients your plants need in their first few months and it will retain its texture indefinitely. Soilless compost can be used in smaller containers where short-lived plants such as annuals are being grown.

As the compost goes into the tub, prod it fairly firmly with the fingers, so that while not solid it will finish up sufficiently compact for roots to work well and will not sink and settle too much after first waterings.

PLANTING

When your container is correctly positioned and filled with compost you are ready to plant (Fig. 11). Many permanent subjects, such as shrubs, are now offered as container-grown specimens, and these can be planted at any time, provided that the rootball is not disturbed during the operation and plenty of water is made available if the early stages of establishment are taking place during warm weather.

Bare-root shrubs (those lifted from open ground) should be planted from late autumn to early spring when they are dormant.

Summer bedding plants should not be put outdoors in their tubs until all danger of frost is past. Late spring is usually safe.

Spring bedding plants, such as wallflowers and polyanthus, along with spring-flowering bulbs, can be planted in their containers as soon as the summer occupants have been removed. You can usually get away with using the same compost for spring bedding as you used for summer bedding if you work in a handful or two of general fertilizer when the second lot is planted. Renew the compost one year after it was put into the container if the plants are temporary occupants.

Do not try to cram too many plants into one container. Spread them out so they have room to grow. Your tub, pot or trough will soon be a mass of colour if you give the plants room to breathe and to establish their roots.

If you are planting bulbs and spring bedding plants in the same container, put the plants in first and the bulbs in last. In wider tubs and pots it is wise to plant something to give a little height in the centre so that a flat display is avoided.

Always water plants in thoroughly immediately after planting.

TOP-DRESSING

Permanent subjects (well, almost permanent) should not be disturbed unless they have obviously outgrown their containers. I am thinking here of shrubs in tubs (plants in pots and small containers can be potted up as they grow). The more permanent occupants of tubs can be helped along if 5–8 cm (2–3 in) of compost is scraped from the surface each spring and replaced with a layer of John Innes No. 3 potting compost.

Fig. 11 Cross section of a tub planted up. Note adequate layer of 'crocks' over drainage holes, over which there may be a layer of leaf mould, with the plants growing in a top layer of compost.

This will give the plants a welcome boost. Retub these plants only when they have obviously become much too big for their containers, and then take great care to avoid disturbing the roots unduly.

WATERING

This is the most crucial aspect of container gardening. *Never* allow the compost in the contrainer to dry right out. In summer it will often be necessary to water twice a day. Give enough water to soak right through the container when the surface of the compost looks dry. Watering will be needed less frequently at other times of year but should still not be neglected. Try to check your containers every day. When you are away on holiday try to persuade a neighbour to water your pots and tubs for you; if no provision for watering is made you will come home to tubs full of straw. Drought is the commonest cause of death among container-grown plants.

FEEDING

However good the compost in your containers, the plants will exhaust the nutrients in a couple of months (particularly through the summer) and so must be given additional feeds.

Liquid fertilizers are diluted in water and will get straight to the roots. Apply a canful to each tub and a pint to each pot every two weeks through the summer to keep your plants in the peak condition and in bloom for as long as possible.

REMOVABLE LINERS

Many local authorities on the Continent have adopted a method of planting up large tubs and boxes which allows these plant containers to look their best at all times. Each plant display, timed, maybe, to be at its best in spring, summer or winter, is put together on the nursery in a wire mesh or sheet steel liner that will just fit inside the permanent container in the street or market square.

These liners are kept in the nursery until the containers need replenishing. When one display has faded, the workmen lift out the liners with the handles provided and lower in the new display. At no time do the containers look tatty – they are constantly of interest.

Here is a technique that can be used at home in the yard or on the patio if you can afford the money to equip yourself with a few liners, and the space to stand them in while they are being stored or planted up and awaiting their turn.

If the liners are made from strong wire mesh, they should be lined with perforated black polythene or sphagnum moss to retain the compost. Both these and the sheet steel type (again equipped with drainage holes) should be treated with exterior quality paint each year.

A layer of drainage material will be needed in the base, and a good compost similar to that used in tubs and window boxes will keep the plants going.

Plant up the reserve liners a few weeks before they will be needed to allow the plants to become established. Wall-flowers, for instance, can be moved directly from the rows in which they were sown into the liners. Here they will be spaced at sufficient distance to allow development, and you will have cut out the need to transplant them to a wider spacing before they are put in their final positions.

You will find the liners particularly useful at the end of summer for

Not all tulips are tall and stately. There are dwarf varieties, too, such as the scarlet 'Fusilier' here emerging through a carpet of pansies.

in some years the display will carry on well into late autumn. You can enjoy it but still not be late with your spring display by having it well underway in another liner.

CLIMBERS

Climbing plants provide a ready means of bringing height to container plantings. They will be happy in ordinary compost but do need support (Fig. 12). A wigwam of 2–m (6–ft) bamboo canes will suit most of them if the container is to be free standing. If it is to be positioned

Fig. 12 Climbers in tubs. Climbers do need support, provided here by a 'wigwam' of bamboo canes.

against a wall, attach trellis-work or horizontal wires to the surface with masonry nails, and lead the stems of the climbers up their permanent supports.

Climbers, in particular, need adequate supplies of moisture so be extra-conscientious about watering.

FOOD CROPS

There is no reason why salad crops, tomatoes and even runner beans should not be grown in containers. The bean makes a delightfully decorative climber which is doubly valuable for its flowers and its pods.

If the containers are close to the house your vegetables will be very easy to harvest in wet weather.

Herbs, too, will be close at hand for kitchen use, and many of them are deliciously aromatic when grown in pots on a warm patio or doorstep.

Strawberries are particularly well adapted to being grown in containers. They can be planted in special strawberry pots, which are rather like oil jars with open pockets spaced at intervals down the sides, or in barrels drilled with large holes in the side to accept them. In such containers the fruits hang down the sides and are cleaner than those grown on the surface of the soil.

Again, watering is critical. Make sure that the compost is never allowed to dry out or your crop will be affected.

CHOICE OF PLANTS

There are many plants which cannot find a successful home in a container, but equally there is a vast range which can. Choice depends purely on personal preference and container capacity. Light and shade inevitably have their influence but, again, there is planting material enough to take care of this.

The lists at the end of the book include shrubs, herbaceous plants, annuals, bulbs and herbs that will thrive in pots, tubs, troughs, urns, oil jars and even wheelbarrows to provide colour and interest the whole year round.

CHAPTER 3

WINDOW BOXES

It seems sensible to give window boxes a chapter to themselves, for they can be used by flat-dwellers who do not have even a doorstep on which to stand a tub or pot, and to whom a patio is no more than a pipe dream.

Not that window boxes should be confined to flats and used only by people who do not possess gardens. Think how much brighter the ordinary street would be if more householders bedecked their sills with flower-filled boxes.

Planted and replanted two or three times a year these containers will provide year-round colour and interest. There are lots of small plants that give of their best in our more inhospitable months, and many of these can be used in window boxes as well as tubs, pots and other containers.

But before we look at the planting up of the window box, a word or two about choice.

CHOOSING WINDOW BOXES

All manner of generously decorated troughs are offered by manufacturers. Some have intricate wrought iron patterns on the front, others brightly painted panels. Some are moulded in relief to offset their otherwise bald appearance, and still more are left plain. Strangely enough the plainest are often the most effective, for they show off the plants to best advantage, rather than detracting from their beauty.

By all means choose a window box whose appearance appeals to you, but think also what it will look like when it is full of plants.

SIZE

The size of your window sill will naturally govern the size of the window box. Choose a box that is not quite as long as your sill so that you can get your hands around the ends to lift it when necessary. Width is similarly governed, but there is no reason why your box should not overhang by an inch or so if it has to. As to depth, aim for a minimum of 20 cm (8 in). This will give the plants enough compost to sink their

Provided they are always kept cool, crocuses seldom disappoint, sending up their purple, white or golden goblets through a shaving brush of leaves. This is 'E. P. Bowles'.

roots into and will also prevent them from drying out too quickly.

Very shallow window boxes will soon become parched in bright sunlight and the plants in them will wilt and be severely checked.

COLOUR

Much depends here on the colour of your existing paintwork, for the box should blend in with it rather than contrast. Many plastic troughs offered for use as window boxes are a brilliant white, and while this is quite likely to blend in with any other colour it does tend to stand out rather too much. What is more it looks grimy very quickly when used in areas where there is even the slightest hint of industrial pollution.

Dull greens, muted browns, and natural finish of varnished wood are, I think, among the most successful shades of window box. Certainly there are instances where white and other bright colours are acceptable – on colourwashed cottages for instance – but muted colours win hands down as a rule.

MATERIALS

Plastic is certainly the longest lasting material, if it is stout enough at the outset. Wrought iron frames containing steel boxes are fine for a few years but the dreaded rust can make short work of them once it gains a foothold. Timber boxes look good, last well if treated with preservative reasonably regularly, and go well with plants.

Glass-fibre is strong and long lasting, and many troughs are available that have been modelled on old lead ones. They are grey and will easily pass for lead from only a few feet away.

HOME-MADE BOXES

There is no reason why a home-made window box, custom-made to fit your own sill, should not last just as long as a comparative version bought from a garden centre or hardware store.

Ordinary deal is quite suitable and can be treated with a timber preservative such as Cuprinol to prolong its life. Exterior quality plywood is suitable, too, as are hardwoods such as oak, but these will naturally be more expensive than ordinary deal.

You do not need a degree in woodwork to construct a window box and I will not stifle your powers of invention by giving you a pattern. All your box needs is a bottom with holes drilled in it at 10–15 cm (4–6 in) intervals to allow drainage of surplus water; two sides and two ends (Fig. 13). They can all be held together with brass screws (if you are a real workmanlike carpenter) or with nails (if you just like to get

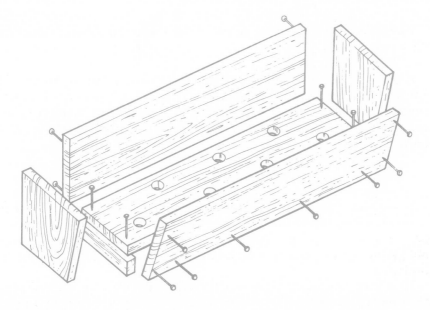

Fig. 13 Making a window box. Exploded diagram showing construction of a simple window box; use timber 1·9–2·5 cm (¾–1 in) thick and remember to drill the drainage holes in the base.

things done quickly). Two pieces of 5–cm by 2.5–cm (2–in by 1–in) timber should be attached to the underside of the box to act as feet and allow excess water to escape freely from the drainage holes.

As soon as you have made your box, give it a coat of preservative inside – a generous coating at that – and allow it to soak in. Outside the timber can be painted with exterior quality clear varnish, or exterior quality paint in a muted shade.

I have a varnished window box on one of my sills that was knocked together with nails four years ago. It has been planted up twice a year ever since and still shows no signs of rot.

If you really want to care for your box, clean it out and give it a fresh coating of Cuprinol and varnish or paint every two years. This will keep it relatively rot-free and always smart.

POSITIONING

Certainly window boxes are at their best on sills that receive a fair amount of sun. But sills in dappled shade can still be brought to life with flower-filled containers.

Like heavy tubs, window boxes are best positioned before they are filled with compost. Staggering to a high sill with a heavy and over-long trough is nobody's idea of a pleasant pastime.

If you lack sills all round your house or flat do not despair. Stout steel brackets fixed to the wall with screws driven into plugs will support troughs of considerable weight (Fig. 14). If you are no handyman (or handywoman) a local builder will be able to put the brackets in place once you have bought your trough.

DRAINAGE

Although drying out is the greatest problem likely to be faced, in winter the compost in the boxes will become extremely soggy if water has no means of escape. All troughs *must* be provided with drainage holes, and if none are present when you buy a trough they must be drilled.

However, rain and constant soakings from the watering can will tend to compact the soil within the trough, so forcing it into the drainage holes in the base and blocking them. For this reason it is advisable to have some protective layer of roughage in the bottom of the box to keep the holes free and to ensure the rapid escape of surplus water.

Broken flower pots, or crocks, are fine if you have them. They can be laid hollow side down over the drainage holes and the compost put directly on top. If you feel that you need to do a 'belt and braces' job, you can place another layer of roughage such as coarse peat, leaf-mould or broken bricks over the layer of crocks to make sure that water will not have a chance of hanging around. If you do not possess any crocks, use broken bricks or a little rubble as the first layer.

COMPOST

Soilless compost (the type based on peat) is fine for about a year and will support a crop of summer bedding followed by bulbs and spring flowers. After such a period of use it can be discarded (on to the garden and used as a mulch) and replaced with fresh mixture.

A better idea is to use loam-based compost such as John Innes No. 2 potting compost, for this has a longer life and can be topped up as necessary rather than completely replaced.

Where a window sill is lacking, strong angle brackets can be used to support a well-filled window box.

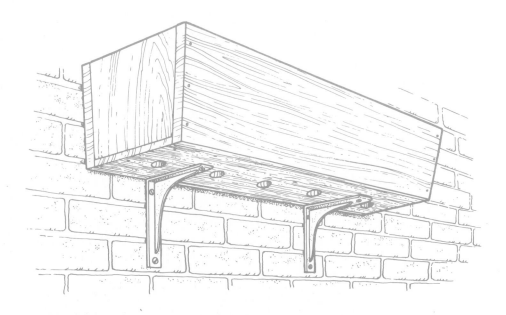

Fig. 14 Supporting a window box where there is no sill. Stout steel brackets properly fixed to the wall will support troughs of considerable weight.

Both composts will supply the plants growing in them wih adequate nutrients in the early stages (the soilless type for about six weeks after planting and the John Innes for rather longer) but then additional feeds will have to be applied if the plants are to continue to perform to their best ability.

Fill the container with compost when it is in position and lightly firm the mixture into place. Planting can then be carried out.

PLANTING

So much of planting is common sense. The plants should be inserted so that neither they nor their roots are unduly cramped, but at the same time they should not be spaced out to look like soldiers. Leave a little room between them to allow for growth, bearing in mind their ultimate size. Take out a generous hole so that the roots will fit easily and not have to be poked into place, and refirm the compost around them. When planted the soil level in their new container should be at about the same height as the soil mark on their stems.

If you want to see out of your window, plant tall specimens towards the sides of the box and short one in the middle. A forest of vigorous plants on your window sill will soon turn your room into a dimly lit cave. A small trowel makes planting easy but there is no reason why you should not use your hand to scoop out the compost which will be loose enough to handle.

When the plants are in place the soil level should be about 2.5 cm (1 in) below the rim of the container to allow for watering. This is *very* important. Bring the level higher and you will not be able to water the container very easily. It is said that 2.5 cm (1 in) of water will travel 23 cm (9 in) down into the soil, so you can see that the gap left between compost and trough rim is critical if all the roots in the container are to be adequately supplied with water.

If you are planting bulbs and plants in the box, do remember to put the plants in first and the bulbs in last. Do it the other way round and you are likely to spear the bulbs when the plants are put in.

WATERING

As with other containers, window boxes should never be allowed to dry out completely. Keep your eye on the surface of the soil at all times and as soon as it shows signs of becoming dry, fill the box to the rim with water and allow it to soak through.

Do not visit the box with the watering can again until the compost once more shows signs of dryness.

FEEDING

After a month or two, the plants in the box will be running out of food. Supplement their diet by giving them additional nutrition in the form of liquid feeds. Many proprietary formulations are available, and if you choose one from the range of a well-known manufacturer you can be confident that your plants will be receiving a balanced diet. Chop and change the feeds if you like, but never make them stronger than the label suggests. One spoon for the pot may be fine as far as your cup of tea is concerned but it will not do your plants any more good than the regulation amounts. If manufactures thought that larger doses would produce big, fit, vivid blooms I have no doubt they would tell us so!

As a rule, liquid feeds can be given once every two weeks through the growing season. Apply the feed just as you would water, but do not wait until the compost is dry. Given to the plants while the compost is moist it will find its way into their sap stream much more quickly.

WEEDING

In spite of your best endeavours, weed will find their way ino the window box and should be pulled out by hand as soon as they are seen. Do not wait for them to become large – they will only compete for light and nutrition with the legitimate inhabitants of the box.

FLOWERS

Bright blooms and attractive foliage might be all you need in your window box, but do not think of this simply as a summer and maybe a spring display. There are plenty of plants that perform well in winter and you can vary your scheme to give colour all the year round. The plant lists at the back of the book will give you plenty of ideas.

VEGETABLES, FRUIT AND HERBS

If you are desperate for lettuce, tomatoes, radishes, chives, marjoram, basil, mint and parsley, they can all be yours with a window box. What is more you do not have to traipse down to the bottom of the garden for them in your mac and wellingtons on a wet day; simply open the window and they are within your grasp.

There is really very little difference in growing these crops in a window box compared with in the garden if you pay attention to watering and feeding.

There is no reason why ledges above windows, as well as below them, shouldn't be used for window boxes provided they are strong and weatherproof.

CHAPTER 4

ROOF GARDENS

Standing on a rooftop has a curious fascination, assuming you have a head for heights. There is a distinct sense of freedom, the sort of freedom you can feel gazing seaward from a clifftop.

Flat-topped roofs, which are accessible and safe to be on, soon find themselves well used. They may become observation platforms, and they are almost certain to give a rise to sunbathing. If they are strong enough there is little doubt that they will soon sport planted pots, boxes, tubs and troughs, as the horticulturist living below realizes what opportunities lie above. A roof garden is in the making.

Individual ingenuity and imagination will influence the development and form of a roof garden, but three of the governing factors will be the actual roof area, its structual strength and all-round safety. Water-proofing, plus arrangements for shedding rainwater will almost certainly be built in. Such may well suffice for the more modest and most likely kind of roof garden to be made; namely, one consisting of a range of planted containers. More grandiose schemes may well call for purpose-built drainage and water-proofing systems.

Thoughts on grand schemes need to take into account ways and means of transporting and hoisting materials through the house to the roof. The weight, water-proofing and drainage factors become particularly relevant, as does disposal of debris through the seasons. Looking at an extensive roof garden on top of one of London stores, for example, albeit a rather large one, with its lawns and borders, does press home these points.

Consultation should take place with the local authority to establish whether a roof garden would be permissible on any roof and to check on the minimum height required for parapets. Many new extensions offering flat roofs and seemingly invitations to make roof gardens are in fact not strong enough, nor surfaced in suitable material. Roofing firms or knowledgeable builders are worth consulting, in order to establish the strength and suitability for roof gardens of flat roofs on both old and new buildings.

Concrete roofs, with their in-built strength, would seem to offer great encouragement to would-be roof gardeners. Stress, containment, drainage and water-proofing factors would all have to be gone into with great care. All the right answers present, the way might be open for lawn sections, beds and borders. Should thoughts about shipping soil in quantity on to any suitable, strong, durable, well-drained roof finally show the idea to be feasible and worthwhile, it would under any circumstances be as well to lay a bed of 8–10 cm (3–4 in) diameter half-pipes over the area chosen for soiling, by way of immediate drainage. This would, of course, increase the stress on the structure.

Access for both working and enjoying any roof garden is a prime consideration. It becomes additionally relevant as the garden becomes more ambitious.

In regard to soil in mass on the roof, there would tend to be a lot of residual moisture, particularly in wet times and seasons of the year. There would certainly be an acute – if temporary – increase in weight when everything in the garden received sudden heavy rain or persistent snowfall, considering the depth of soil required to sustain growth in simulated garden conditions. A dry cubic yard of soil weighs something in the region of a ton. Soaking wet it will obviously be considerably more. Held wet over an extended winter period it would exert prolonged and extra stress. Seepage problems could become likely here.

Soilless composts are much lighter than their loamy counterparts, of course, and though plants growing in them will need feeding more frequently through the summer they are well worth considering.

ROOFTOP CONTAINERS

The chances are that the majority of roof gardens will be made up of adroitly positioned and thoughtfully chosen containers. Given a sound, reasonably level roof, sturdily water-proofed (probably with asphalt) and provided with proper drainage gullies and ports, a roof with an adequate parapet all round and which is easily accessible from the house, the roof gardener is on his way.

In order to capitalize on maximum roof strength, plant containers should be positioned reasonably close to supporting walls where strength will be greatest. This is not so important with light pots and tubs, but certainly applies to the bulkiest of containers.

If ornamental slabs or tiles are used to create interest here and there, the lightweight asbestos-cement tiles are available from builders' merchants and garden centres. Stuck down with mastic adhesive they can help to transform otherwise less exciting asphalt without adding too much extra burden to the roof.

There are tubs and rigid plastic pools enough to make the creation of a water feature a possibility, but weight and strategic positioning become more vital than ever. Pool cleaning (let alone overflow in response to wet weather) must also be remembered. Efficient water-proofing and drainage would be vital. Do not consider having a roof pool unless both you and your roof can take it.

Speaking of water, there needs to be provision of a water supply for the care of rooftop plants – quite apart from pool filling and topping up. Such considerations should be given early in order to make sure that roof garden plants will not die of thirst. You may simply have to resort to lugging heavy watering cans up the stairs!

It is usual to jack containers clear of the surface on which they are standing, in order to allow drainage water which has filtered through after they have been watered to run away freely. This is additionally important in a roof garden situation, not just for the sake of the plants in their containers, but also for the roof surface which is likely to suffer if water lies trapped between it and the container bottom. It may also become raised in the vicinity of the container if there is insufficient circulation of air underneath during hot times too.

CHOICE OF CONTAINER

It would seem wise to choose containers which are as light as possible, but yet durable and of good design. The more weight that can be saved the better. Just a little thought needs to go into container profile. It is no good choosing those which are too shallow, for they will hold too little planting compost and be more than likely to suffer rapid drying out, especially on windy or exposed rooftops. On the other hand, something of a low profile would seem to be an advantage in windy places, or where there might not be a great deal of parapet protection. Plants in such containers would be less likely to suffer buffeting. Note that the larger each individual container, the larger amount of compost taken to fill it and therefore the greater the concentrated weight in one given roof spot.

If there is a convenient wall or chimney stack, such as can be found on top of some of the tall-storied London houses, there is every encouragement to install wall pots in ornamental brackets, or suspend hanging baskets.

I came across a highly successful garden some years ago, high on a roof in London. Here were containers of all kinds, including wall pots. A trellis supported climbing plants, and bamboos cunningly laced together provided shelter from the wind.

Trailing lobelia masks the front of this trough, pink-flowered pelargoniums grow in the centre and black-eyed Susan, *Thunbergia alata*, grows up the sides of the window.

WIND PROTECTION

The problem of wind may call for early consideration. Screens acting as filters are valuable. Wattle hurdles filter wind very effectively and look attractive into the bargain. All screens need to be firmly fixed if they are not to take off in high winds, but this should cause few problems, especially if the screens are of sensible proportions.

Prevailing winds are always likely to affect arrangement and style within roof gardens. Screening and trellis sections, for example, should be introduced to achieve maximum protection with the minimum resistance. The positions of screening and trellis determined, the garden with its grouped and distributed containers can then be formed in the best possible way. Protection as a first move is one of the main keys to success.

Much depends on area, but container or trellis colour is worth a little thought, depending on how much grime there is in the atmosphere. Pristine white may not be a good idea. Paints and finishes need to be durable for containers, trellis, screens and furniture on very exposed rooftops.

CHOOSING THE PLANTS

Precise planting selections will be made by the individual, but if these are made from durable species then success is more likely to result. Lots of the standard bedding plants and annuals survive well in roof gardens; particularly enjoying the benefit of wind-breaking screens. As to permanent plants, it is worth giving a thought to the kind which are low growing or normally able to withstand more windswept conditions and a certain degree of drying out.

Sun beating back from an asphalt surface or from walls in a confined rooftop circumstance can create the kind of conditions that arise on a sun-trap patio, and the plants mentioned in the lists given at the end of the patio section (and, indeed, in the container and window box sections) are likely to thrive in rooftop situations. Steer clear only of those which are of considerable stature and therefore offer a lot of resistance to wind.

Finally, perhaps, choose some garden furniture for lightness, durability and, above all, comfort – you can then sit back on a sunny day and enjoy your roof garden to the full.

CHAPTER 5

PESTS AND DISEASES

The secret of keeping pests and diseases at bay lies in growing your plants well. Healthy, vigorous specimens will be able to shrug off attack far more readily than those which are dry at the roots, pot-bound or starved. But however well you grow your plants there will be some pests that will almost certainly put in an appearance. When they do you must act fast and stamp out the infestation before it has time to gain a firm foothold.

By growing a wide range of plants you will be less likely to suffer devastating attacks of uncommon pests and diseases; it is the more widespread types that will give you headaches.

The following list indicates the problems you are most likely to encounter.

ANTS

Fast-moving and ubiquitous insects, too well known to need description. Can be troublesome on sitting-out areas; they milk aphids for honeydew, so encouraging their presence.
Contol: Pour boiling water on to nests (only partially effective). Lay poisoned baits containing borax which insects will take back to nests, so affecting rest of colony.

APHIDS (Greenfly and blackfly)

These honeydew-secreting insects may attack a wide range of plants, sapping their vigour and causing their leaves to become coated with sticky exudate. Aphids also spread virus diseases.
Control: Spray with pirimicarb, malathion or derris.

BIRDS

Pigeons and sparrows are the main problem in town gardens, though blackbirds may occasionally be a nuisance. Tender shoots, buds and fruits may be wholly or (more annoying still) partially eaten.

Control: Many repellent sprays are only effective until the first shower of rain. Netting is really the only certain means of preventing attack but it may be too unsightly. Try rigging up some sort of scaring device using bright strips of foil, but change the position (and if possible, the design!) every few days so that the birds do not become accustomed to the warnings. Serious trouble is likely to be encountered only in spring when shoots are tender and the birds short of food; or in winter and autumn when fruits are ripe.

BLACKLEG

This type of grey mould, or botrytis, which attacks pelargoniums

When plants are put in as thickly as this there's no way the container can be seen (handy if it's a plastic bucket) but adequate drainage holes plus watering and feeding are essential.

Large-flowered varieties of petunia which are so often damaged by heavy rain are often protected from heavy downpours on a window sill.

(geraniums) causing the stems to turn black at the base before the plant wilts and dies.
Control: Grow the plants in sterile compost. Root cuttings in a well-drained medium and ventilate well.

BLACKSPOT

A disease of roses in which the leaves become covered in black spots which eventually converge to form larger black areas.
Control: Pick off and burn any infected leaves to stop the fungal spores from spreading. Spray with bupirimate and triforine or Benlate. Clear away and burn all fallen leaves in autumn.

CLEMATIS WILT

Apparently healthy shoots suddenly wilt and wither. Entire stems may collapse and occasionally the whole plant is affected.

Control: Cut out and burn all infected stems. Drench the soil surrounding the plant with a solution of Benlate. Plants will usually recover.

FROGHOPPER

More commonly known as cuckoo spit, this pest is more of a nuisance than an enemy, for its protective coating of spittle can mess up your clothes.
Control: Spray the plants with water to disperse the spittle and then the spray with malathion to kill the pest.

GREY MOULD

Leaves and stems of many plants may become soft and rotten before being covered in a grey furry outgrowth. Correctly known as botrytis.
Control: Remove all infected parts of the plant. Grow well and make sure that sufficient food and water is available at all times. Do not overcrowd the plants.

LEAFMINER

Chrysanthemums, roses, cinerarias and one or two other ornamental plants may become infested with this pest which burrows into the leaf tissue leaving behind it a white tunnel pattern.
Control: Spray with malathion in the early stages of attack.

MICE

Bulbs and corms may suffer from the depredations of mice.
Control: Traps are safer than poisoned baits.

MILDEW

Particularly common on roses, mildew causes the leaves and stems to become coated in a white powdery layer which later turns grey and causes the tissue to rot.
Control: Remove and burn any badly infected stems. Spray with bupirimate and triforine or benlate.

RED SPIDER MITE

These tiny mites (no bigger than a pin-prick) suck sap from plants,

particularly on the undersides of the leaves, causing them to become pale and bleached.
Control: Spray with malathion or dimethoate.

SCALE INSECTS

Brown scale may attack a wide range of plants but it is particularly keen on those which have rather glossy leaves. It sucks the sap and secretes messy honeydew.
Control: Wash off the scales with a piece of cottonwool dipped in diluted malathion or methylated spirits.

SLUGS

Slugs *and* snails can make mincemeat out of a wide range of plants, eating both flowers and leaves.
Control: If you do not have any domestic pets, lay poisoned baits in the form of pellets. Where there are pets, use a liquid slug killer. Alternatively grapefruit skins turned hollow-side downwards can be used to trap the pests.

THRIPS

Leaves and flowers become speckled with silvery-grey spots due to sap being suckled. Flowers may be streaked and disfigured.
Control: Spray severe infestations with gamma-HCH.

VIRUSES

Leaves may be mottled with yellow, distorted or generally weak and lacking in vigour. Flowers may be malformed and small. There are many virus diseases and most of them are spread by insects such as sap-sucking aphids.
Control: Pull up and destroy any infected plants. Do not propagate from infected stock.

WOODLICE

These insects usually confine themselves to attacking dead and decaying matter, but they can also eat plant roots, stems and leaves.
Control: Trap the insects as you would slugs in half grapefruit skins. Keep the patio and other areas free of fallen leaves and other debris.

An otherwise stark house front becomes a hanging garden thanks to a myriad of pots and bowls and baskets that cheer its countenance.

APPENDIX:
A–Z OF PLANTS TO
GROW IN CONTAINERS

Shrubs, hardy perennials, annuals and even one or two small trees are included in this list. Plan the content of your containers carefully and you can enjoy flowers and foliage the whole year round.

KEY

Types: Column 2

HHA	— Half-hardy annual
HP	— Hardy perennial
S	— Shrub
B	— Bulb
TP	— Tender perennial
T	— Tree
HB	— Hardy biennial
CI.S	— Climbing shrub
A.CI	— Annual climber

Containers for which plants are suitable: Column 8

P	— Pots
T	— Tubs
WB	— Window boxes
HB	— Hanging basket
S	— Sink garden

Plant	Type	Description
Acer palmatum varieties (Japanese maple)	T	Small deciduous trees with finely cut leaves of green or maroon. Good autumn colour.
Agapanthus 'Headbourne Hybrids'	B	Long stems carrying rounded heads of dark or light blue flowers. Green strap-shaped leaves in summer.
Ageratum varieties (floss flower)	HHA	Fluffly flower heads of blue, pinkish blue or white. Coarse green leaves.
Alyssum varieties (sweet alyssum)	HHA	Small mounds or trails of white or pink flowers. Sweetly scented.
Anemone De Caen or St. Brigid	B	Large double or single flowers of red, white, blue or pink, each with a central black 'eye'.
Antirrhinum varieties (snapdragon)	HHA	Tall or short spikes of red, yellow, pink, white, orange or magenta blooms.
Aster varieties	HHA	Bushy annuals with double or single daisy flowers in shades of red, pink, mauve, purple and white.
Aubrieta deltoidea (purple rock cress)	HP	Trailing rock plants with small flowers of crimson, purple, pink or white carried in large numbers.
Aucuba japonica 'Variegata' (spotted laurel)	S	Large, glossy evergreen leaves which are green spotted with yellow.
Begonia semperflorens	HHA	Small glossy-leaved annuals. Foliage may be green or dark brown; flowers red, pink or white.
Begonia (tuberous varieties)	TP	Large green leaves and large double or single blooms of red, orange, yellow or white.
Bellis perennis 'Monstrosa' (double daisy)	HP	Small tufts of green leaves from which arise crimson, pink or white daisy flowers.
Betula pendula 'Youngii' (Young's weeping birch)	T	Small mushroom-headed tree with weeping branches, small green leaves and 'silver' bark.
Buxus sempervirens (box)	S	Dense shrubs with small evergreen leaves. Can be hard clipped to make pleasing designs.

Height (when container-grown)	Planting season	Season of interest Flowers	Foliage	Particularly suitable for:
up to 2 m (6 ft)	Late autumn– early spring	—	Spring–Autumn	T
60 cm (2 ft)	Early – mid-spring	Summer	Spring–Autumn	T, P
15–30 cm (6–12 in)	Late spring	Summer	—	P, T, WB, HB
10 cm (4 in) trailing	Late spring	Summer	—	P, T, WB, HB
23 cm (9 in)	Mid-autumn	Summer	—	P, T, WB
20–30 cm (8–12 in)	Late spring	Summer	—	P, T, WB
23–30 cm (9–12 in)	Late spring	Summer	—	P, T, WB
Trailing	Late autumn	Spring	—	T, WB, S
1–2 m (3–6 ft)	Late autumn – early spring	—	All year round	T
15 cm (6 in)	Late spring	Summer	—	T, P, WB, HB
30 cm (1 ft) or pendulous	Late spring	Summer	—	T, P, WB, HB
15 cm (6 in)	Early – mid-autumn	Spring	—	T, P, WB
3m (10 ft)	Late autumn – early spring	—	Spring–Autumn	T
up to 1 m (3 ft) if clipped	Early – mid-spring	—	All year round	T, P

Plant	Type	Description
Calluna vulgaris (heather, ling)	S	Small fuzzy-foliaged plants of value both for their purple, red or white flowers and the coloured foliage many of them possess.
Camellia varieties	S	Large evergreen shrubs which carry large red, pink, white or contrastingly striped blooms in spring.
Celosia argentea 'Pyramidalis'	HHA	Bright red, orange or yellow plumes are carried at the top of the central stem.
Centaurea gymnocarpa	HHA	Finely cut grey leaves which are useful as a foil for more brightly coloured plants.
Centranthus ruber (red valerian)	HP	Generous heads of pink or white flowers carried at the ends of the stems.
Cerastium tomentosum (snow in summer)	HP	An extremely vigorous trailing plant with grey leaves and white flowers. Rampant.
Chaenomeles varieties	S	Deciduous shrubs with bright blossom of pink or scarlet.
Chamaecyparis lawsoniana 'Lutea Nana'	S	A slow-growing conifer with yellow-green foliage.
Cheiranthus varieties (wallflower)	HB	Too well known to need description. Scented flowers come in shades of red, orange and yellow.
Chionodoxa luciliae (glory of the snow)	B	Tiny sprays of blue and white flowers held among narrow green leaves.
Clematis varieties	Cl.S	A tremendous variety of plants to choose from with large blooms of blue, purple, white, pink and red. Deciduous.
Cleome spinosa (spider flower)	HHA	An elegant annual with spiky flowers of pink.
Cobaea scandens (cup and saucer vine)	A.Cl	A climbing annual with bell-shaped white blooms which turn purple as they age.
Coleus varieties (flame nettle)	HHA	Bushy plants with brightly coloured leaves which may be marked with crimson, pink, orange and yellow.
Continus coggygria 'Foliis purpureis' (smoke tree)	S	A deciduous shrub with rounded deep purple leaves. An excellent contrast for bright flowers.

Height (when container-grown)	Planting season	Season of interest Flowers	Foliage	Particularly suitable for:
15 cm (6 in)	Late autumn	Summer–Winter	All year round	T, P, WB, S
up to 2 m (6 ft)	Autumn or Spring from pots	Spring	All year round	T
30 cm (1 ft)	Late spring	Summer	—	T, P, WB
60 cm (2 ft)	Late spring	—	Summer–Autumn	T, P, HB
60 cm (2 ft)	Late autumn	Spring–Summer	—	T, P
Trailing	Late autumn	Spring–Summer	—	T, WB
2 m (6 ft)	Late autumn	Spring	—	T
Eventually 2 m (6 ft)	Mid-spring	—	All year round	T
30 cm (1 ft)	Mid-autumn	Spring–Summer	—	T, P, WB
15 cm (6 in)	Early – mid-autumn	Spring	—	T, P, WB, S
4.5 m (15 ft)	Mid – late autumn	Spring–Autumn	—	T
1 m (3 ft)	Late spring	Summer–Autumn	—	T, P
3 m (10 ft)	Late spring	Summer–Autumn	—	T
30 cm (1 ft)	Late spring	Summer–Autumn	—	T, P, WB
2 m (6 ft)	Late autumn – early spring	Summer–Autumn	Summer–Autumn	T

Plant	Type	Description
Cotoneaster salicifolius	S	An evergreen shrub which carries white flowers followed by red berries.
Crocus varieties	B	Small bulbous flowers of purple, orange, lilac, yellow or white.
Elaeagnus pungens 'Maculata'	S	An evergreen shrub with oval leaves blotched yellow in the centre.
Erica varieties (heath)	S	Small fuzzy-leaved shrubs with crimson, purple, pink, or white flowers. Many have orange or yellow foliage in winter.
Fatsia japonica (false castor oil)	S	Large, glossy, green, hand-shaped leaves are carried all year round on a stately plant. White flowers in autumn.
Forsythia intermedia	S	Bright yellow starry flowers are carried before the leaves emerge. Deciduous.
Fuchsia varieties (tender types)	TP	Bushy or more pendulous deciduous shrubs with dainty pendulous flowers of white, pink, crimson and purple.
Gazania varieties	HHA	Large daisy flowers of orange, red, yellow and white.
Hebe pinguifolia 'Pagei'	S	Dwarf evergreen shrub with grey leaves and small white flowers.
Hedera helix varieties (ivy)	Cl.S	Green or variegated leaves are carried the whole year round. The plants will climb or trail.
Helianthemum varieties (rock rose)	S	Mound-forming or trailing evergreen shrubs with rounded flowers of white, yellow, orange or red.
Heliotropium varieties (heliotrope)	HHA	Large heads of purple flowers. Scented.
Hibiscus syriacus varieties	S	Late-leafing and flowering shrubs with large blooms of crimson, pink, blue or white.
Hosta species & varieties (plantain lily)	SP	The bold leaves which emerge in spring may be blue-grey, green, green and white or green and yellow. White or lilac flowers arise later.
Hyacinthus varieties (hyacinth)	B	Pink, blue, white, yellow, orange or red 'drumsticks' of scented flowers.

Height (when container-grown)	Planting season	Season of interest Flowers	Foliage	Particularly suitable for:
2 m (6 ft)	Late autumn – early spring	Summer (berries in Autumn)	All year round	T
10 cm (4 in)	Late summer – mid-autumn	Autumn– Spring	—	T, P, WB, S
2 m (6 ft)	Late autumn – early spring	—	All year round	T
15 cm (6 in)	Late autumn	All year round (depending on variety)	All year round	T, P, WB, S
2 m (6 ft)	Early spring	Autumn	All year round	T, P
3 m (10 ft)	Late autumn – early spring	Spring	—	T
up to 1 m (3 ft)	Late spring	Summer– Autumn	—	T, P, WB, HB
23 cm (9 in)	Late spring	Summer	—	T, P, WB
23 cm (9 in)	Late autumn – early spring	Summer	All year round	T, P., WB
Will climb to any height if supported	Late autumn – early spring	—	All year round	T, WB, HB
30 cm (1 ft)	Late autumn	Spring– Summer	—	T, S
45 cm (18 in)	Late spring	Summer– Autumn	—	T, P
1.25 m (4 ft)	Late autumn – early spring	Late summer	—	T
60 cm (2 ft)	Late autumn – early spring	Summer	Spring–Autumn	T, P
30 cm (1 ft)	Early – mid-autumn	Spring	—	T, P, WB

Plant	Type	Description
Hydrangea macrophylla varieties	S	Deciduous shrubs with massive flower clusters of pink, white or blue.
Ilex altaclarensis 'Golden King' (holly)	S	A relatively slow-growing holly with yellow variegated leaves. It carries berries in autumn.
Ipomoea varieties (morning glory)	A.Cl	Climbers bearing large trumpets of pink. mauve or blue.
Juniperus varieties (juniper)	S	The low-growing junipers have feathery foliage of blue or green carried on spreading horizontal stems.
Lathyrus varieties (sweet pea)	A.Cl	Fragrant flowers of white, blue, pink, crimson, or maroon.
Laurus nobilis (bay)	S	Dark evergreen leaves. Most attractive when grown as a clipped specimen.
Lavandula varieties (lavender)	S	Grey-leaved, blue-flowered aromatic shrubs which make rounded domes of foliage.
Lilium regale (regal lily)	B	Tall, elegant lilies with white and yellow flowers flushed maroon on the outside.
Lobelia varieities	HHA	Trailing annuals with blue, white or carmine flowers.
Lonicera periclymenum (honeysuckle)	Cl.S	Trailing stems which are covered with spidery flowers of pink and yellow in summer. Scented. Deciduous.
Lysimachia nummularia 'Aurea' (creeping Jenny)	HP	A trailing plant with yellow flowers and bright yellow rounded leaves.
Magnolia soulangeana	S	An evergreen shrub which carries large, cup-shaped blooms of white, flushed purple in spring.
Mahonia aquifolium	S	An evergreen shrub with bronze-green pinnate leaves and tassels of yellow flowers.
Mesembryanthemum criniflorum (Livingstone daisy)	HHA	Trailing annual with bright daisies of white, orange, magenta, pink and red.
Muscari armeniacum (grape hyacinth)	B	Small blue flowers carried on sturdy stems among long green leaves.

Height (when container-grown)	Planting season	Season of interest Flowers	Foliage	Particularly suitable for:
2 m (6 ft)	Late autumn– early spring	Summer	—	T, P
2 m (6 ft) if pruned	Early spring	Autumn (berries)	All year round	T
2 m (6 ft)	Late spring	Summer	—	T, P
1 m (3 ft)	Mid-spring	—	All year round	T, P, S
2 m (6 ft)	Late spring	Summer	—	T
60 cm (2 ft)	Mid-spring	—	All year round	T, P
2 m (6 ft)	Late autumn– early spring	Summer	All year round	T, P
1.25 m (4 ft)	Mid-autumn	Summer	—	T, P
8 cm (3 in) trailing	Late spring	Summer	—	T, P, WB, HB
3 m (10 ft)	Late autumn– early spring	Summer	—	T
Trailing	Mid-spring	Summer	Spring–Autumn	T, P, WB, HB
3 m (10 ft)	Late autumn– late winter	Spring	—	T
1.25 m (4 ft)	Late autumn– early spring	Spring	All year round	T
Trailing	Late spring	Summer	—	T, P, WB, HB
23 cm (9 in)	Mid-autumn	Spring	—	T, P, WB, S

Plant	Type	Description
Narcissus varieties (including daffodil	B	A tremendously varied group of bulbs with yellow, orange and white flowers. Dwarf species suitable for sink culture.
Nemesia varieties	HHA	Bushy plants with white, yellow, orange, and red blooms carried in profusion.
Nicotiana varieties (tobacco plant)	HHA	Tall or short annuals with arching stems of white, green, yellow or red flowers.
Pelargonium varieties (geranium)	TP	Red, pink, magenta or white flowers and green or multicoloured leaves often with a dark zone.
Petunia varieties	HHA	Trumpet flowers in shades of pink, purple, magenta, red, yellow and white.
Picea glauca 'Albertiana Conica' (dwarf spruce)	S	Conical slow-growing conifer with green needles.
Pieris japonica	S	An evergreen shrub with coppery young growths and clusters of white bell-shaped flowers.
Primula (polyanthus)	HB	Compact plants with rosettes of green leaves and primrose flowers of blue, red, orange, yellow, pink or white.
Pyracantha coccinea 'Lalandei' (firethorn)	S	An evergreen shrub carrying dark green leaves and white flowers followed by scarlet berries.
Rhododendron varieties (including azaleas)	S	Deciduous or evergreen shrubs in great variety. Flowers may be red, pink, white purple, crimson, magenta, orange, or yellow.
Ribes sanguineum (flowering currant)	S	Drooping flower clusters of rich pink, followed by pungent green leaves. Deciduous.
Rosa varieties (rose)	S	Deciduous shrubs in tremendous variety. Floribundas and hybrid teas are suitable for container-growing.
Runner bean	A.Cl	Worth growing for its pink, white or scarlet flowers as well as its crop of beans.
Salpiglossis varieties	HHA	Trumpet-shaped blooms of blue, red, yellow or white marked in the throat with a contrasting shade.

Height (when container-grown)	Planting season	Season of interest Flowers	Foliage	Particularly suitable for:
10–45 cm (4–18 in)	Early – mid-autumn	Spring	—	T, P, WB, S
30 cm (1 ft)	Late spring	Summer	—	T, P, WB
30–45 cm (1–1.5 ft)	Late spring	Summer–Autumn	—	T, P
30 cm (1 ft)	Late spring	Summer–Autumn	Summer–Autumn	T, P, WB, HB
23 cm (9 ft)	Late spring	Summer	—	T, P, WB, HB
60 cm (2 ft)	Mid-spring	—	All year round	T, P
1.25 m (4 ft)	Late autumn–late winter	Spring	All year round	T
15 cm (6 in)	Early – mid-autumn	Spring	—	T, P, WB
3 m (10 ft)	Late autumn–early spring	Summer (berries Autumn)	All year round	T
60 cm–2 m (2–6 ft)	Late autumn–late winter	Spring – Summer	All year round	T
2 m (6 ft)	Late autumn–early spring	Spring	—	T, P
1.25 m (4 ft)	Late autumn–early spring	Summer–Autumn	—	T, P
2 m (6 ft)	Late spring	Summer	—	T
45 cm (18 in)	Late spring	Summer	—	T, P, WB

Plant	Type	Description
Salvia varieties	HHA	Stocky plants with scarlet or purple blooms held over green leaves.
Saxifraga varieties (saxifrage)	HP	The mossy or cushion-forming saxifrages are ideal for sink gardens. They have red, pink, white, yellow or purple blooms.
Sedum spectabile (stonecrop)	HP	Large, flat, pink heads of bloom held on succulent grey-green leaves.
Senecio cineraria (dusty miller)	HHA	Deeply cut grey downy leaves. Bushy plants. A good foil for bright flowers.
Sempervivum species (houseleek)	HP	Succulent starry green rosettes, often tipped with maroon or covered with 'cobwebs'. Carpeting.
Syringa vulgaris (lilac)	S	Shrub or small tree with white, lilac or pale purple blooms. Deciduous.
Tagetes varieties (African or French marigold)	HHA	Tall or short bushy plants with single or double flowers of orange or yellow.
Thymus species (thyme)	HP	Creeping, mat-formating plants with small white, lilac or purple flowers. Aromatic. Evergreen.
Tropaeolum varieties (nasturtium)	HHA	Trailing or climbing annuals with yellow, white, orange or red trumpets and round green leaves.
Tulipa varieties (tulip)	B	Cup-shaped blooms of white, pink, red, brown, yellow, orange, lilac, purple. Often constrastingly marked.
Verbena varieties (vervain)	HHA	Annuals of a bushy habit or trailing, with red, pink, purple or white flowers.
Viola varieties (pansy)	HB	Too well known to need description. Flowers may be red, yellow, orange, blue, white. Often marked with deep purple.
Weigela florida 'Variegata'	S	Deciduous shrubs with pink bell-shaped flowers and cream and green variegated leaves.
Yucca species	S	Spiky rosettes of stiff leaves carried eventually on tall stems.
Zinnia varieties	HHA	Bushy annuals with bright double blooms of red, mauve, orange, yellow, white or green.

Height (when container-grown)	Planting season	Season of interest Flowers	Foliage	Particularly suitable for:
30cm (1 ft)	Late spring	Summer	—	T, P, WB
10 cm (4 in)	Late autumn	Spring–Summer	—	T, P, WB, S
45 cm (18 in)	Late autumn–early spring	Autumn	Summer	T, P
30 cm (1 ft)	Late spring	—	Summer–Autumn	T, P, WB, HB
2.5 cm (1 in)	Mid-spring	Summer	All year round	T, P, WB, S
3m (10 ft)	Late autumn–early spring	Summer	—	T
15–45 cm (6–18 in)	Late spring	Summer	—	T, P, WB, HB
Creeping	Late autumn–early spring	Summer	All year round	T, P, WB, S
2 m (6 ft) or trailing	Late spring	Summer	Summer	T, P, WB, HB
15–45 cm (6–18 in)	Mid–late autumn	Spring	—	T, P, WB, S
15 cm (6 in) or trailing	Late spring	Summer	—	T, P, WB, HB
15 cm (6 in)	Early–mid-autumn	Spring	—	T, P, WB,
1.25 m (4 ft)	Late autumn–early spring	Summer	Spring–Autumn	T
1.25 m (4 ft)	Late autumn–early spring	Summer–Autumn	All year round	T, P,
30 cm (1 ft)	Late spring	Summer	—	T, P, WB

INDEX